SHABBAT
AND THE
MODERN KITCHEN

SHABBAT AND THE MODERN KITCHEN

By Rabbi L.I. Halpern
English edition by Rabbi Dovid Oratz

Copyright © Gefen Publishing House, Ltd.
Jerusalem 1986/5746

All rights reserved. No part of this publication may be translated, reproduced, stored in a retrieval system or transmitted, in any means, electronic, mechanical, photocopying, recording or otherwise, without express written permission from the publishers.

Typeset: Gefen Publishing House, Ltd.

ISBN 965-229-021-1

First Edition 1986
Edition 9 8 7 6 5 4

Gefen Publishing House, Ltd.
P.O.B. 6056, Jerusalem
91060 Israel
(02) 380-247

Gefen Books
12 New St., Hewlett
N.Y., U.S.A. 11557
1(800) ISRL BKS

Send for your FREE Catalogue of Books from Israel

Printed in Israel

TABLE OF CONTENTS

Introduction	I
Preface	IX
Foreward	VIII

SECTION I
Modern Heat-Sources and the Prohibitions of Shabbat

Introduction		11
Chapter 1	Bishul and *mechaze Ki-mevashel*	13
Chapter 2	Shehiyah and Chazarah	15
Chapter 3	The conditions for Prohibition of chazarah	25
Chapter 4	Does the Prohibition Remain if Stoking does not apply?	29
Chapter 5	Modern Food-Warming Devices on Shabbat	35
Chapter 2 Appendix	— Proof that the Prohibition of Chazarah is Based upon "Stoking"	47

SECTION II
Automatically Heating Food on Shabbat

Introduction		59
Chapter 1	Automatic Cooking and Gerama	61
Chapter 2	A "Preparatory Cooking Act"	65
Chapter 3	Using an Electric Time Clock for Shabbat	69
Chapter 4	Automatic Cooking and *mechaze Ki-mevashel*	75
Chapter 5	Automatic Cooking and "Stoking the Coals"	77
Chapter 6	Reheating Fully Cooked Liquids	83
Chapter 7	A System for Automatically Heating Food on Shabbat	87

SECTION III
An Alternate System for Re-heating Food on Shabbat

Introduction		95
Chapter 1	*Kli Sheni*	97
Chapter 2	Placing Pots of Food into a *Kli Sheni*	103
Chapter 3	A Warming Bath for Reheating Food on Shabbat	105

SECTION IV
Reheating Food for Hospital Patients

Introduction		111
Chapter 1	*Gerama* of Cooking in a Hospital	113
Chapter 2	Is Hot Metal Considered "Fire?"	117
Chapter 3	The Views of the *Chashmal Le'or HaHalakha* Regarding Whether Hot Metal is Considered Fire	121
Chapter 4	Hot Metal as a "Solar Derivative"	131
Chapter 5	A System for Heating Food on Shabbat for Hospital Patients	137
Chapter 6	An Alternate Solution for Heating Hospital Food	139

SECTION V
The Thermostat in Refrigeration and Heating

Introduction		149
Chapter 1	Thermostatic Systems	151
Chapter 2	Affecting the Thermostat and *Pesik Reisha*	153
Chapter 3	Actions that Lengthen an Existing Status	157
Chapter 4	Conclusion	159

SECTION VI
Hot Water Systems

Introduction		169
Chapter 1	General Hot Water Systems	171
Chapter 2	Hot Drinking Water	177
Chapter 3	Coffee and Tea Machines	189
	Summary	195

Introduction

"I believe with total belief that this Torah will not be changed..."[1] is the ninth of the Rambam's (Maimonides) Thirteen Basic Tenets of Judaism. By extension, the precepts of the Torah that "will not be changed" must be eternal. Accordingly, the precepts of Shabbat, the "Eternal Covenant" between Yisrael and God,[2] apply to the twentieth century just as they applied at Sinai.

Much technological progress has been made in the many centuries that elapsed from the time that the Torah was given at Sinai, specifically in this last century. Since the Torah is eternal, this progress should in no way mitigate the applicability of the precepts of Shabbat to the life-style of today. Nevertheless, this progress raises several important questions.

Among these questions is how the Torah prohibitions of doing work on Shabbat relates to the modern methods of food preparation. Although the Torah does not directly define the term "work" (*Melakhah*), our Sages explain that the types of work done to construct the Tabernacle are the types of work prohibited on Shabbat. They derive this from the fact that the Torah prefaces the section that discusses the construction of the Tabernacle by saying, "Six days shall work be done... whoever does work on it (Shabbat) shall be put to death."[3] Accordingly, the thirty-nine types of work done to construct the Tabernacle are considered the archetypes for prohibited Shabbat work.[4]

But is activating a heating element equivalent to the category of work, kindling fire (*Havarah*)? Does cooking in a seemingly fire-free oven transgress the prohibition of cooking (*Bishul*)? Reheating food in a food warming bath? A steam kitchen? Would these transgress the Rabbinic prohibition of "Appearing as cooking"? Do the cooking related Rabbinic prohibitions aimed at preventing the likelihood of stoking the coals apply to modern non-coal fuels for which "stoking" is unnecessary? Is it appropriate to establish a new prohibition that would apply to modern fuels just as "stoking" applied to ancient fuels? What occurs when an electrical circuit is closed? Perhaps the fact that closing a circuit transforms an inactive mass of wire and metal into an active machine means that the category of work, building *(Boneh)* is involved?

More generally: Can circumstances be arranged before Shabbat so that work be *automatically* done on Shabbat? If so, can an object be placed on Shabbat where it will subsequently be acted upon automatically? Does it matter whether or not the Shabbat placer and the one who arranged the circumstances before Shabbat are different people?

What about indirect causation? If the result of some action (e.g. opening the door of an oven) is to close a circuit that causes Shabbat work to be done, (e.g. the thermostat closes the heating circuit) is that action different than directly doing the Shabbat work? Does it matter what the intention of the action was? What if the result of the action was removing a barrier so that an action could result?

The answers to these questions are important in their own right, but assume even greater importance in their application to hospitals and similar institutions. These institutions must serve fresh hot food for medical reasons. If such institutions want to strictly follow the Halakhah, then the answers to these questions would indicate what technical modifications of their systems had to be made to enable preparation of Halakhically acceptable hot food.

The extenuating circumstances usually involved in hospitals differ from the circumstances generally involved in normal settings. Nevertheless, eating hot food on Shabbat is considered so important a part of the Joy of Shabbat (*Oneg Shabbat)* that "one who refrains from eating hot food (on Shabbat) must be checked for apostasy."[5] Accordingly, it is in the spirit of *Oneg Shabbat* to determine the various methods that may be used to prepare hot food for Shabbat.

This book attempts to determine the various methods that modern technology makes available to prepare Halakhically acceptable hot food on Shabbat. This is done through carefully analyzing the above questions, among others, in light of the Halakhic literature. This analysis clearly shows that not only does science and the modern way of life not conflict with Halakhah, but that they may be used to serve the goals of Halakhah. It is hoped that this book will be an aid in understanding the Halakhot of Shabbat in general, and specifically how relevant they are in the modern world. Through this understanding, may we come closer to the point of "If Yisrael would observe two Shabbats (*Shabbatot*) the Redemption would immediately come."[6]

1. *Rambam*, Thirteen Basic Tenets of Faith
2. Ex. 31:16
3. Ex. 35:2
4. TB Shabbat 49b; *Rashi* s.v. *"K'Neged"*
5. *Hama'or Hakatan,* Shabbat III s.v. *"V'Im Tish'al"; Mishnah B'rurah* 257:49
6. TB Shabbat 118b

Preface

The publication of *Kashrut Ve'Shabbat Ba'Mitbah Hamoderni* added an important dimension to the Halakhic literature. This literature had always dealt with technological change by analyzing how the immutable principals of Halakhah apply to the innovations of technology. *Kashrut Ve'Shabbat Ba'Mitbah Hamoderni* follows this tradition, but also demonstrates how technology may be used to serve the needs of Halakhah by developing systems that are acceptable and even desirable from a Halakhic viewpoint. It was written in a fashion that could be understood on two levels: The simple lay level that describes the Halakhically acceptable technological solution, and the advanced level that analyzes the Halakhic issues in depth.

Despite the obvious interest that the non-Hebrew speaking world would have in such a book, direct translation would be of little value. Whereas the first level could easily be translated, a translation of the telegraphic style used in Halakhic studies would leave most readers as mystified as they would be by the original Hebrew. Indeed, any reader that could follow all the various allusions and nuances, could presumably have followed the original Hebrew.

On the other hand, increasingly sophisticated Halakhic works in the English language have educated the non-Hebrew speaking public. Accordingly, if the Halakhic material would be clearly developed and expanded upon in English, then anyone interested in investing the necessary time and effort could follow the logic. This book is an attempt at presenting the Shabbat section of *Kashrut Ve'Shabbat Ba'Mitbah Ha'Moderni* in such a manner.

In any language the book is the work of Rabbi Halperin and those at the Institute for Science and Halakhah who helped him. My work involved trying to understand how his conclusions were reached so that they could be clearly developed and presented in English, as well as applied, where possible, to matters not discussed in the book. As part of this work it was necessary to spend countless hours discussing the material with Rabbi Halperin and to retranslate anything I wrote into Hebrew, so that even the nuances could be approved by him. Thus, the development, presentation, and some applications of the Halakhah is my work with Rabbi Halperin's approval; the Halakhic conclusions, and the basic Halakhic structure, fully the work of Rabbi Halperin.

This book shows the Halakhic process in action. It can be used to further develop an appreciation for that process, and to learn the basic Halakhot relating to food preparation on Shabbat. *It cannot be used as a basis for independent Halakhic conclusions.* the complexity of the fine differentiations that must be made between seemingly similar cases, and wealth of information that must be examined before a valid Halakhic conclusion can be reached, should leave such conclusions exclusively to competent Rabbis. On the other hand, knowing what and how to ask is also important.

I am greatly indebted to Rabbi Halperin for the privilege of learning from him, and for the countless hours that he spent with me to help prepare this book. I am similarly indebted to my teacher and mentor, Rabbi Tuvia Goldstein, Rosh Yeshiva of Beit Midrash Emek Halakhah, who is responsible for giving me the background and tools for handling material of this nature. I would also like to thank Rabbi Moshe Chait, Rosh Yeshivah of the Yerushalyim branch of Yeshivat Chafetz Chaim, for encouraging me to write at a crossroad in my life. I am forever indebted to my parents and my in-laws for all that they have done and continue to do for me.

A special thank you to the following people: To my good friend, Joseph Fridman, whose patience and encouragement are responsible for this book. To Joey Epstein, who did much to improve the flow and clarity of the book. To Chaim Friedberg, who helped clarify several important technological points. To Rabbi Chaim Septimus, who offered some valuable suggestions.

Most important of all, to my wife, Adele, who encouraged me at every point and took care of our home and family like a true *Eshet Hayil*. In addition to this indirect help, she, more than anyone else, read and reread each draft that I wrote and made many insightful comments and corrections. These immeasurably improved the clarity of the Halakhic issues and the stylistic flow of the entire book. Words cannot express my gratitude to her. May God reward her by granting her wish (and mine): That our children become *Talmidei Hakhamim*.

DOVID ORATZ
Yerushalyim, Adar 5746

The Halakhic research for this book was made possible through the generous help of the Jesselson Family.

Foreward
by Rabbi Dr Samson R Weiss

The present volume is an important addition to the realm of halachic literature. It is an English translation of part of a rather intricate study called 'Kashruth and Shabbath in the Modern Kitchen', (written, of course, in Hebrew and) replete with terms and idioms germane to the close reasoning of the Halachist, dealing with a variety of problems arising from modern kitchen installations and their use by Torah observing institutions and individuals.

While the original work, as its title indicates, treats also Kashruth questions, this translation limits itself to the problems of food preparation and food warming for and on the Shabbath, culling the pertinent chapters from the original and reorganizing their sequence in a manner conducive to its more narrow scope. Such reorganization of the contents of the original (often) was also necessary, to serve the purpose of this translation, within the individual chapters. As Rabbi Dovid Oratz, the translator, indicates in his Preface, this 'translation' consitutes in many respects also an original halachic treatise. New nuances and new halachic aspects are herein developed. While based on the original and fully approved by its author Rabbi Levi Yitzchak Halperin, these are still the fruit of the translator's own halachic competence.

Rabbi Levi Yitzchak Halperin, the author of 'Kashruth and Shabbath in the Modern Kitchen', probably is today's leading halachic authority on scientific and technological innovations as they affect the Halach in its practical aspects. The head of the Department of Halach of the 'Institute for Science and Halacha', he is the recipient of inquiries from Rabbanim and Dayanim from all parts of the Jewish world, as well as from Jewish hospitals and other public institutions in Eretz Israel and in the lands of our dispersion. His fertile literary output, books, essays and articles, has earned him a well deserved place in the front row of contemporary halachic authors.

The purpose of this work is to introduce the reader to the fascinating, rich fabric of halachic reasoning and its terminology. If it evokes his desire to progress to the study of Hebrew original, it will have served an additional dimension of 'Limud Torah'.

SECTION I

Modern Heat-Sources and the Prohibitions of Shabbat

Introduction		11
Chapter 1	Bishul and *mechaze Ki-mevashel*	13
Chapter 2	Shehiyah and Chazarah	15
Chapter 3	The conditions for Prohibition of chazarah	25
Chapter 4	Does the Prohibition Remain if Stoking does not apply?	29
Chapter 5	Modern Food-Warming Devices on Shabbat	35
Chapter 2 Appendix	—Proof that the Prohibition of Chazarah is Based upon "Stoking"	47

Introduction

The technological innovations of the twentieth century caused sweeping changes in the food warming process. These changes include new and different fuels, novel forms of stoves and ovens, and a diversity of innovative devices that function as heat maintainers. The question therefore arises: To what degree do these changes in the food-warming devices affect the applicability of the various cooking-related prohibitions of Shabbat?

These prohibitions include the Torah prohibitions of *Bishul* and the Rabbinic prohibitions of *Shehiyah, Chazarah,* and *mechaze Ki-mevashel,* (also called *Nireh Ki-mevashel*). Each of these prohibitions will be discussed and analyzed with respect to modern food warming devices. Chapter one discusses the prohibitions of *Bishul* and *mechaze Ki-mevashel,* and shows that for these prohibitions, no differentiation can be made between older and newer food warming devices. Chapter two discusses *Shehiyah* and *chazarah* and indicates that the reason for these prohibitions may not apply to modern food warming devices. Appended to chapter two is a complex chapter that proves that the reason for prohibiting *chazarah* is the same as the reason for prohibiting *Shehiyah*. Chapter three discusses the circumstances that prohibit *chazarah* because of *mechaze Ki-mevashel*, and by extension, when the conclusions of chapter two do not apply. Chapter four proves that when the reasons for prohibiting *Shehiyah* and *chazarah* do not apply, the prohibitions do not apply as well. Chapter five applies the conclusions of the first four chapters to modern food warming devices and introduces new information upon which to base a Halakhic conclusion.

Chapter 1
Bishul and *mechaze Ki'mevashel*

Bishul refers to the Torah prohibition of cooking on Shabbat. It is transgressed when a liquid is brought to a given temperature as a result of fire-related heat, and when an uncooked solid changes its physical properties as a result of being cooked a certain amount over fire-related heat.[1] This change is said to occur when the food is cooked to *Ma'akhal Ben Derusai*, either one third[2] or one half[3] cooked.

"Fire-related heat" is the only external factor relevant to *Bishul*. Cooking the required amount with fire-related heat transgresses the prohibition of *Bishul*, regardless of the fuel or specific device involved. Gas heat, in which fire is fueled by gas, is, therefore, equivalent to any other fire-related heat. Even electric heat is considered by most authorities fire-related, because of the red-hot metal coils that produce the heat.[4] Thus, cooking the required amount in modern gas or electric warmers on Shabbat transgresses the prohibition of *Bishul*, just as cooking the required amount in traditional coal stoves and ovens does.

Related to the Torah prohibition *Bishul* is the Rabbinic prohibition *mechaze Ki-mevashel*, appearing as cooking. Once a solid food (as opposed to liquids, see Section II, Chap.6) is fully cooked, recooking does not transgress a Torah prohibition.[5] It is, nevertheless, Rabbinically prohibited to place any food in an oven in which *Bishul* would normally result for uncooked food. Since the viewer does not know that the food involved is fully cooked solid food, such placement "appears as cooking." A placement that "appears as cooking" is Rabbinically prohibited.[6] Accordingly, placement of fully cooked solid food upon any modern heating device that would otherwise transgress the Torah prohibitions of *Bishul*, transgresses the Rabbinic prohibition of *mechaze Ki-mevashel*.

Thus, any modern food warming device that is fire-related and brings food to a given temperature can transgress the prohibitions of *Bishul* on Shabbat. Placing fully cooked solid food on such warmers "appears as cooking" and is Rabbinically prohibited. Since gas and electric warmers meet these criteria, the prohibitions of *Bishul* and *mechaze Ki-mevashel* seem to apply to them as they do to traditional food warmers.

Chapter 2
Shehiyah and Chazarah

I. *The Mishnah of Kirah*

The two Rabbinic prohibitions that seem problematic in application to modern food-warming devices are *Shehiyah* and *chazarah*. *Shehiyah* refers to leaving food over fire on Shabbat, and *chazarah* refers to re-placing food onto fire on Shabbat. The ramifications of these prohibitions and the reasons behind them constitute some of the most complex rulings of Shabbat. To facilitate analysis of their applicability to modern food warming devices, a discussion of the Talmudic basis for these prohibitions is necessary.

The Talmudic basis for these prohibitions is the Mishnah that states:
"A *Kirah* [portable stove of Talmudic times. See figure 1] fueled by straw may have a cooked pot placed upon it; [fueled by] peat or wood, [a cooked pot] may not be placed, until he sweeps [the coals], or places ash [banks the coals]"[7]

This Mishnah is the subject of much controversy, the most fundamental of which, for our purposes, is the definition of the Mishnaic term "placed" (*Yiten*). There are two apparent ways of defining "placed." The simplest, most literal definition, is "placed on Shabbat." An alternate definition is "placed before Shabbat and allowed to remain upon the heat source on Shabbat."

Despite the simplicity and literalness of the first definition, it is untenable. The prohibition of placing cold food onto a heat source on Shabbat is universally accepted (see Chapters 1 and 3) regardless of whether or not "he sweeps or places ash." The Mishnah, therefore, cannot possibly permit placing a pot of food on Shabbat onto a *Kirah* whose coals are swept or covered with ash.

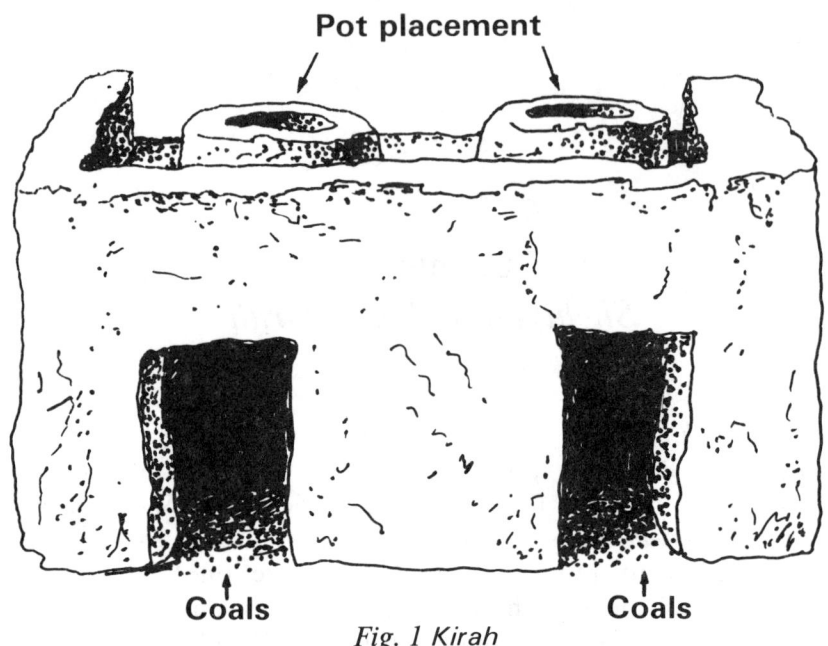

Fig. 1 Kirah

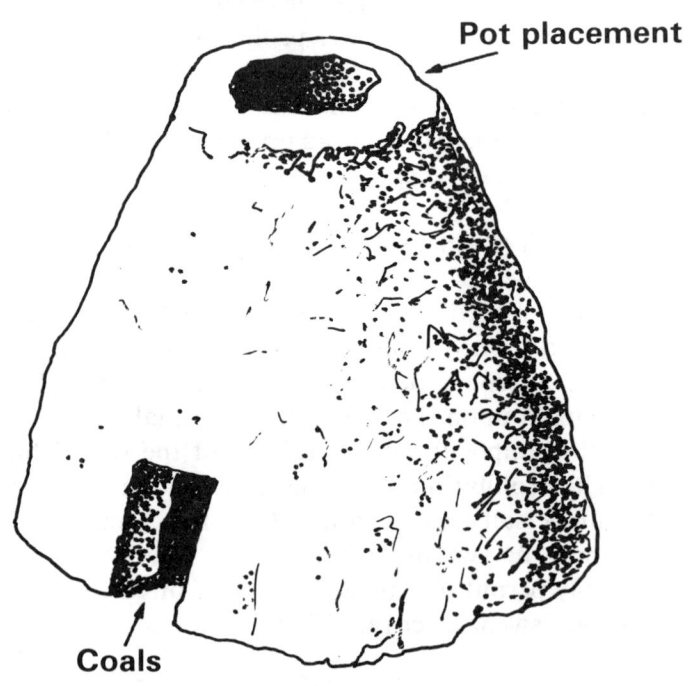

Fig. 2 Tanur

The second alternative is also somewhat problematic. If "placed" is defined as "placed before Shabbat and allowed to remain upon the heat source on Shabbat" (which is also the definition of *Shehiyah*) then the conclusion seems to be that *Shehiyah* is only permitted when the coals of the fire are swept or covered with ash. Since this section of the Mishnah is uncontested, there would appear to be Halakhic concurrence with that conclusion. Yet, Chananiah, a Mishnaic authority, is cited by the Talmud as permitting *Shehiyah* over an open fire for food that is at least *Ma'akhal Ben Derusai* (one third or one half cooked).[8] This ruling is also not explicitly contested, thereby also implying Halakhic concurrence.

Rather than conclude that Chananiah contests this seemingly uncontested Mishnaic ruling, the Talmud proposes an alternate definition for "placed:" "re-placed on Shabbat." According to this definition, the Mishnah rules that food removed from a *Kirah* may be re-placed on Shabbat (*Chazarah*) only if the coals of the *Kirah* were swept or covered with ash.[9]

The Talmud fails to conclusively support this proposal, and remains undecided between this definition and the previous definition. The Halakhic ramifications of the two definitions are quite different. If "placed" is defined as "placed before Shabbat and allowed to remain upon the heat source on Shabbat," then, as mentioned above, *Shehiyah* would only be permitted when the coals of the fire are swept or covered with ash. *Chazarah* would have the same ruling, in accordance with the Halakhically accepted ruling of Beit Hillel cited in the continuation of the Mishnah.[10] If "placed" is defined as "replaced on Shabbat," then whereas *chazarah* would be permitted only when the coals of the fire are swept or covered with ash, *Shehiyah* (of *Ma'akhal Ben Derusai*) would be permitted even without sweeping the coals or covering them with ash, in accordance with the ruling of Chananiah.

The *RaMA*, one of the foundations of Ashkenazic Halakhah, rules that this more lenient ruling may be practiced.[11] Accordingly, food that is half-cooked or more may remain on an open flame on Shabbat. The more recent *Biur Halakha* (written by the author of the *Mishnah Brurah*) however, indicates that it is preferable not to rely on this lenient ruling.[12] Wherever possible, therefore, *Shehiyah* is permitted only when the coals are swept or covered with ash. As to *chazarah*, all agree that it is only permitted when the coals are swept or covered with ash.[13]

But that is the ruling for a *Kirah*. How does this ruling apply to modern food-warming devices? What is the equivalent of "coals" that must be "swept or covered with ash"? Indeed, why must the coals of a *Kirah* be swept or covered with ash? Does that reason apply to modern food-warming devices?

II. *"Stoking the Coals"*

Rashi and *Tosfot*, the Talmudic commentaries of the Rishonim era printed in the margins of the Talmud, cite conflicting reasons why the coals of a *Kirah* must be swept or covered with ash before "placing" is permitted. The reason given by *Rashi* seemingly applies to modern food-warming devices, whereas the reason given by *Tosfot* may not. *Rashi* explains that coals "add heat. The reason [for requiring sweeping or covering with ash] being, as explained in the previous chapter (TB Shabbat 34B), to prevent stoking the coals."[14]

The page referred to by *Rashi* discusses the prohibitions of *Hatmanah,* fully surrounding a pot of food (even before Shabbat) in a heat-generating substance. It explains that *Hatmanah* is prohibited to prevent the likelihood of surrounding a pot with live coals. Since coals tend to extinguish unless they are periodically stoked, surrounding with live coals could result in stoking the coals to increase the heat. Such stoking would transgress the Torah prohibition of *Havarah* (burning fire). The basis for the Rabbinic prohibition of *Hatmanah,* therefore, was to prevent the likelihood of transgressing a Torah prohibition.

Rashi seems to consider "placing" into a *Kirah* whose coals are neither swept nor covered with ash, a sub-case of *Hatmanah*. "Placing" onto a *Kirah* whose coals are swept or covered with ash is permitted, presumably because the coals no longer generate heat. *Tosfot* rejects this view. He points out that coals covered with ash generate more heat than many other substances with which *Hatmanah* is prohibited. Thus, if "placing" is a sub-case of *Hatmanah*, then sweeping or covering with ash should not mitigate the prohibition. Furthermore, Chananiah, who as previously indicated, permits *Shehiyah* of *Ma'akhal Ben Derusai* without sweeping or covering with ash (in which case the coals certainly generate heat), also prohibits *Hatmanah* with substances that generate heat. Thus, the prohibitory factor for *Shehiyah* must differ from the prohibitory factor for *Hatmanah*. This prohibitory factor, concludes *Tosfot*, is the "prevention of the likelihood of stoking the coals (*Gezerah Shema yechateh b'gechalim*)".[15]

To explain: Both *Rashi* and *Tosfot* agree that the ultimate reason for prohibiting *Shehiyah* (*Tosfot* does not discuss *chazarah*) is to ensure that the Torah prohibition that results from stoking the coals on Shabbat is not transgressed. *Tosfot* considers this the direct reason for the prohibition. *Rashi* on the other hand, uses the intermediate step of considering *Shehiyah* a sub-case of *Hatmanah*. The difficulties resulting from the intermediate step caused *Tosfot* to reject the view of *Rashi*.

Rabbi E.M. Hurwitz, a nineteenth century Talmudic commentary, defends the view of *Rashi*. He agrees that *Rashi* could not possibly have considered "placing" a sub-case of *Hatmanah*. Rather, both "placing" and *Hatmanah* have a common prohibitory factor: preventing the likelihood of stoking the coals. The lenient factors for "placing," however, need not match the lenient factors for *Hatmanah*.[16]

This approach seems to indicate a basic practical difference between the views of *Rashi* and *Tosfot*. *Rashi*, who compares "placing" to *Hatmanah*, can consider *Hatmanah* an apt model for "placing." *Hatmanah* is prohibited in heat-generating substances for which "stoking" does not apply, as a preventive measure against the likelihood of *Hatmanah* in live coals for which "stoking" does apply. Similarly, "placing" should be prohibited regardless of the specific applicability of "stoking," barring those circumstances explicitly exempted from prohibitions (coals swept, covered, etc.). *Tosfot*, on the other hand, bases the prohibition directly on the likelihood of "stoking." Where "stoking" is inapplicable, there would seemingly be no prohibition.

If "stoking" could be shown to be inapplicable to a modern food-warming device, that device would seemingly illustrate the difference between *Rashi* and *Tosfot*. *Rashi* could view *Shehiyah* on such a device as analogous to *Hatmanah* in a non-fire, heat-generating substance which is prohibited despite the inapplicability of "stoking" to that substance. *Tosfot*, however, would seem not to prohibit *Shehiyah* on a device for which "stoking" is inapplicable.

The reason given by *Tosfot* for prohibiting *Shehiyah* is the reason cited by virtually all later commentaries and codes.[17] Thus, *Shehiyah* on a device for which "stoking" is inapplicable would seem permissable.

III. *"Swept or covered"*

Before the applicability of "stoking" to modern food-warming devices can be analyzed, the concept of "stoking the coals" must be further clarified. Specifically, why are *Shehiyah* and *chazarah* permitted when the coals of a *Kirah* are swept or covered with ash? Do those actions prevent the likelihood of "stoking?" Indeed, what is meant by "sweeping the coals?" To where must they be swept?

RaMBaM,[18] *RaMBaN*[19] and *RaShBA*,[20] three great commentaries of the Rishonim era, base their answer to the last question on a passage in the Jerusalem Talmud which requires sweeping the coals "completely".[21] They interpret this as requiring the coals to be completely swept out of the *Kirah* — removal — before "placing" is permitted. Removing the coals clearly obviates the likelihood of stoking them.

This interpretation can be questioned from one of the differences between the *Kirah* and the *Tanur* stoves. A *Kirah* is a rectangular, box-like stove, upon which there is room for two pots. A *Tanur* is a stove whose walls slope upwards from a broad, coal filled bottom, to a narrow top, upon which there is room for only one pot (See figure 2). This slope concentrates the heat from the many coals on the large bottom to the area upon which the pot is placed. Due to this heat concentration, some of the rulings pertaining to a *Tanur* differ from those pertaining to a *Kirah*. Among these differences is the Talmudic ruling that prohibits "placing" a pot on a *Tanur* even if the coals are swept[22] (unlike the lenient ruling for a *Kirah*). The question therefore arises: if "sweeping" the coals implies complete removal of the coals, why may a pot not be "placed" upon a *Tanur*?

The *RaMBaM* answers that the great heat of the *Tanur* mitigates the likelihood of removing every last ember. Since these remaining embers might be "stoked" to increase the heat, "placing" on a *Tanur* is prohibited. By implication, if it were certain that no embers could possibly remain, the *RaMBaM,* would rule leniently.[18]

An alternate answer is presented by the *RaMBaN* and the *RaShBA*. In their view, the intense heat of a *Tanur* even after removal of the coals, could mislead the viewer to assume that glowing coals are, in fact, generating that heat. The viewer could further assume that he, too, may "place" his pot on a *Kirah* whose coals are unswept. To prevent the likelihood of that occurrence, "placement" onto a swept *Tanur* is prohibited, even if it were certain that no embers could possibly remain.[19] [20]

The *RaN*, another major commentary of the Rishonim period, asks one question on this answer and another question that applies to this answer as well as to this previous answer. Firstly, how can "placement" onto a *Tanur* be prohibited to prevent the likelihood of "placement" onto an unswept *Kirah*, when that itself is prohibited to prevent the likelihood of "stoking" the coals. Generally speaking, Rabbinical prohibitions were instated only to prevent the likelihood of the direct transgression of a Torah precept (such as "stoking the coals" which increases the fire). Prohibiting "placement" onto a *Tanur*, therefore, should be inappropriate, since the prevented direct result (according to the *RaMBaM,* and *RaShBA*) is only "placement" onto an unswept *Kirah* — also a Rabbinical prohibition.

Secondly, the very basis for the two answers, that the coals must be completely swept out to permit "placement," is incomprehensible. The Talmud permits "placing" a pot upon a *Kirah* whose coals had been covered with ash — even after coals subsequently burst into flame.[23] The Talmud also permits "placing" a pot onto a *Kirah* whose coals dim on their own, even if no ashes were placed on the coals.[24] The *RaShBA* himself explains that covering coals with ash (despite later occurrences), or "placing" a pot over dimmed coals and not "stoking" them back to life, is a clear indication that greater heat is not desired.[25] If greater heat is not desired, then "stoking" the coals is unlikely and "placement" is permitted. According to this explanation, which seems to be the explanation accepted by the Halakha,[26] total removal of the coals should be unnecessary. Any indication that greater heat is not desired should permit "placement."

Because of these two questions, the *RaN* rejects the definitions given by the *RaMBaM, RaMBaN* and *RaShBA* for "sweeping completely." He chooses, instead, the definition given by *Rabbi Zerachiah Halevi*, a contemporary of the *RaMBaN* also known as the *Ba'al HaMa'or*.[27] According to this definition, "sweeping completely" means that all the coals must be swept completely — to the side. This would serve as an indication that further heat is unnecessary, thereby obviating the likelihood of "stoking." Such sweeping would not be sufficient to permit "placement" on a *Tanur*, due to the great heat of a *Tanur*.[28] Nevertheless, if *all* the coals would be removed from a *Tanur*, placement would be permitted.

To summarize the views of the Rishonim as they relate to "sweeping" and covering with ash: The *RaMBaM, RaMBaN* and *RaShBA* require sweeping all the coals out of a *Kirah* to permit "placement," whereas the *RaN* and *Rabbi Zerachiah HaLevi* require only sweeping the coals away from where the pot is placed. Both views seemingly agree that any indications that further heat is unnecessary would obviate the need for a prohibition that prevents the likelihood of "stoking." Accordingly, when the coals dim of their own accord, and certainly when they are covered with ash, "placement" onto a *Kirah* is permitted.

The views diverge again concerning the coals of a *Tanur*. *Rabbi Zerachiah HaLevi* and the *RaN* permit "placement" on a *Tanur* whose coals had been completely removed, since "stoking" is impossible. The *RaMBaN* and the *RaShBA* prohibit "placement" even on such a *Tanur* to prevent the mistaken use of an unswept *Kirah*, in which case the coals might be "stoked." The *RaMBaM,* disagrees with this last point and seemingly permits "placement" onto a *Tanur* whose coals were completely removed. Nevertheless, since he considers complete removal from a *Tanur* unlikely, he prohibits "placement" on any *Tanur*. "Placement" on devices other than a *Tanur*, in which there are no coals to be stoked, however, is seemingly permitted by him.

The view of the *RaMBaM,* is the accepted view cited in subsequent Halakhic codes.[29] Thus, the determinant factor for prohibition is whether or not the coals are likely to be "stoked." Accordingly, when "stoking" the coals is impossible, "placement" should be permitted. If it can be shown that stoking is inapplicable to modern food-warming devices, then "placement" should be permitted. (See appendix to chapter 2 for proof that the prohibition of *chazarah* is also based upon "stoking".)

Chapter 3
The conditions for Prohibition of *chazarah*

It has been demonstrated that the prohibitions of *Bishul* and *mechaze Ki-mevashel* apply equally to all heating devices, while the prohibitions of *Shehiyah* and *chazarah* seem to apply only to those heating devices for which it is necessary to prevent "stoking." This point is further developed in the appendix to chapter 2 with reference to *chazarah*. Nevertheless, it will become apparent that the term *chazarah* is used to cover two prohibitions. The first, as previously discussed, is based upon preventing "stoking." The second, is based upon *mechaze Ki-mevashel*, and applies to all heating devices. It is, therefore, necessary to clearly differentiate between the two prohibitions in the category of *chazarah*. Through this differentiation it will become clear which type of *chazarah* applies to all heating devices, and which applies only when "stoking" need be prevented.

The Talmud implies this differentiation by ruling that even after sweeping the coals or covering them with ash, *chazarah* is permitted only so long as the food is held. "But if he places it [the food] on the ground, it [*chazarah*] is prohibited."[30] Based upon this ruling, the *Shulchan Arukh* concludes:

"A pot removed from a *Kirah* [whose coals were] swept or covered may be re-placed even on Shabbat as long as it is boiling" [adds the *RaMA*: "and still in his hand"] "and he did not place it on the ground" [adds the *RaMA*: "and his intention was to re-place it"].[31]

Clearly, these conditions do not affect the likelihood of "stoking." Furthermore, the coals of the *Kirah* are swept or covered with ash. Thus, these conditions cannot be to prevent the likelihood of "stoking."

The commentary of the *Rosh* on the unanswered Talmudic query concerning the permissibility of Chazarah of food after transfer to another vessel[32] (see chapter 5:II) clarifies the reason for these conditions. The *Rosh* questions why the ruling for *Hatmanah* (see chapter 2) is more lenient for food transferred to another vessel, whereas the ruling for *chazarah* seems more stringent after transfer to another vessel. To strengthen the question he points out that, in general, the rulings for *Hatmanah* are more stringent than those for *chazarah*. His answer differentiates between the applicability of the reasons for the general prohibitions of *Hatmanah* and *chazarah* to this specific case:

"... we prohibit *Hatmanah* from nightfall, to prevent the possibility of *Bishul* [by bringing the food to a boil]. When he transfers, this does not apply since would he cool it now [through transfer] if he wanted to boil it? However, when he re-places here [the second vessel] onto the hot *Kirah* we ask if that [the transfer] is comparable to placing it on the floor, thereby cancelling the original *Shehiyah*, and it would be like a new placement, and he would [appear to] cook on Shabbat."[33]

"Cancelling the original *Shehiyah*." This explains why the conditions listed in the *Shulchan Arukh* are necessary to permit *chazarah* on a *Kirah* whose coals are swept or covered with ash. The lack of any of these conditions "cancels the original *Shehiyah*." It then appears to be a new placement which "appears as cooking" and is thus prohibited.

In effect these conditions delineate when a placement act can be defined as *chazarah*. If the conditions are met, then the placement is *chazarah* and it is permitted on a *Kirah* whose coals are swept or covered, as a continuation of the original *Shehiyah*, but prohibited when "stoking" is likely. If the conditions are not met, then the action cancels the original *Shehiyah* and cannot be considered proper *chazarah*. Accordingly, it is prohibited on any heating device because it "appears as cooking."

In summation: strictly speaking the term *chazarah* refers to replacing food under specific conditions. Such re-placing is prohibited to prevent the likelihood of "stoking," unless that likelihood is mitigated. If the specific conditions are not met, the re-placement is still loosely referred to as *chazarah*. This type of re-placing, however, appears to be a new placement, and is prohibited because it "appears as cooking." The former type of *chazarah* should be permitted on a heating device for which "stoking" does not apply (as discussed in chapter 2 and 4), whereas the latter type is prohibited on any device for which *Bishul* applies (as discussed in chapter 1).

Chapter 4
Does the Prohibition Remain if Stoking does not apply?

One important factor remains to be proven. It has hitherto been assumed that whenever the stated reason (prevention of "stoking") for a prohibition (*Shehiyah* or *chazarah*) does not apply, the prohibition is nullified. Generally speaking, however, the seeming inapplicability of the reason for a prohibition does not, of necessity, nullify the prohibition. For example: taking medication on Shabbat (for illnesses that are not serious) is Rabbinically proscribed to prevent the possibility of grinding medicinal herbs on Shabbat, which transgresses a Torah prohibition.[34] Although the reason applies more to a time in which each individual ground his own medicine, than to modern times, the prohibition is nevertheless not nullified.[35] It is, therefore, necessary to prove that where "stoking" does not apply, *Shehiyah* and *chazarah* are permitted.

The first proof that where "stoking" does not apply *Shehiyah* and *chazarah* are permitted, is derived from the prohibition to read by the light of an oil lamp on Shabbat.[36] The Tosefta, auxilliary writings of the Mishnaic period, explains the prohibition as a preventive measure against the possibility of tipping the lamp when the light begins to dim. Tipping the lamp brings additional oil to the wick, thereby causing a brighter flame, and involving the Torah prohibition of *Havarah* (burning fire). The Tosefta applies this prohibition to a lamp ten stories away as well, despite the improbability of tipping the lamp ten stories away.[37]

Nevertheless, later authorities discuss later types of lamps for which tipping is inapplicable, by whose light, they feel, reading is permitted. One example of such a "lamp" is a wax candle whose steady flame obviates the necessity of "tipping."

The *Hagahot Asheri,* a commentary on the *Rosh* of the late Rishonim period, questions whether the inapplicability of tipping a candle would permit reading by candlelight on Shabbat.[38] Although he does not answer this question, the *Beit Yosef,* author of the *Shulchan Arukh,* concludes: "it seems clearly prohibited to me, since he could possibly trim or cut the top of the wick [which can involve at least partial extinction of the flame]."[39]

This conclusion of the *Beit Yosef* has important ramifications. In his view, the specific inapplicability of the reason for prohibition does not nullify the prohibition when some other reason for prohibition exists. Accordingly, *Shehiyah* and *chazarah* onto a heating device for which "stoking" is inapplicable could be prohibited as a preventive measure against, for example, extinguishing the fire when the food is ready.

On the other hand, the *Bach,* a seventeenth century commentary on the *Beit Yosef,* rules that candlelight may be used for all Mitzvah purposes. The prohibition, in his view, "applies only to an [oil] lamp called 'Kreizal.' But with our candles, there is no fear of tipping."[40]

The *Magen Avraham* cites both views in his early eighteenth century commentary on the Shulchan Arukh. He questions the ruling of the *Beit Yosef,* since even if the top of the wick were trimmed, and even if the fire were extinguished, no Torah prohibition is transgressed. If no Torah prohibition is transgressed, it is inappropriate to make a preventive measure.[41] The *TaZ,* a contemporary of the *Magen Avraham*, concurs and raises an additional question on the ruling of the Beit Yosef:

If there could be a prohibition based upon trimming, why did the Tosefta base the prohibition on tipping? It should have used the more basic, more inclusive reason that applies to all wick-containing light. The fact that the Tosefta ignored the seemingly more universal reason, implies that the Tosefta does not accept the validity of that reason. Therefore, concludes the *TaZ,* reading by candlelight should be permitted.[42]

Among the later codes and commentaries, the *Shulchan Arukh HaRav,* an eighteenth century codification, cites both views and permits reading by candlelight "in time of need." He explains that the difficulty involved in trimming the wick of a candle obviates the need for Rabbinic proscription.[43] The *Mishnah B'rurah,* an early twentieth century commentary on the *Shulchan Arukh,* is even more lenient. He asserts that modern candles are never tipped nor are their wicks ever trimmed. He, therefore, concludes that even the *Beit Yosef* would permit reading on Shabbat by the light of modern candles.[44]

Another example of a "lamp" that differs from the oil lamp is the kerosene lamp. The *Misgeret HaShulchan,* a nineteenth century commentary, explains that kerosene lamps burn with consistent brightness from the time that they are lit until the time that the kerosene is consumed. In this respect, it differs from an oil lamp that burns inconsistently and requires tipping for the wick to burn more brightly. Accordingly, he concludes that a kerosene lamp is an acceptable light source for reading on Shabbat.[45] The *Biur Halakha,* written by the author of the *Mishnah B'rurah* rules that this view may be relied upon for Mitzvah purposes, or when other lenient circumstances are involved, specifically since the wick of a kerosene lamp is glass enclosed.[46]

Many other authorities, however, question the permissibility of the kerosene lamp, or any other lamp in which the wick is glass enclosed. In their view, the glass is comparable to a wick ten stories away, which the Tosefta prohibits.[47] Nevertheless, the *Eliyahu Rabah*[48] and later authorities assert that all would permit reading by such light if the glass covering were locked and the key held by another person. In that case, the key-holder, who is not involved in reading to the exclusion of all else, would remind the reader that it is Shabbat.[49] The *Biur Halakha* suggests that a note on the lamp stating that it is Shabbat is the functional equivalent of the key being held by a second person.[50]

Why these lenient rulings when the Tosefta prohibits even a light ten stories away? The original prohibition applied to oil lamps, and rather than finely differentiate between permitted and prohibited circumstances, all reading by the light of oil lamps was prohibited, even when the light is ten stories away. However, for light sources other than oil lamps the determinant factor for prohibition is whether or not the reason for prohibition applies.

This discussion may be summarized as follows: The Rabbinic prohibition of reading by lamplight seems to apply specifically to light that decreases of its own accord. Accordingly, many authorities permit reading on Shabbat by light that does not decrease of its own accord, specifically if other lenient factors are present. Although the *Beit Yosef* prohibits reading by candlelight because of the possibility of trimming the wick, most authorities disagree. They do not consider the possibility of trimming the wick sufficient cause for prohibition, either because no Torah prohibition is transgressed when trimming or because the difficulty of trimming obviates the necessity for prohibition. All seemingly permit reading by a light for which neither tipping nor trimming are applicable.[51]

Thus, *Shehiyah* and *chazarah* onto a heating device for which "stoking" does not apply should certainly be permitted. Lamp light was prohibited for all circumstances, and yet many permit non-oil lamps for which the reason for the prohibition does not apply. *Shehiyah* and *chazarah* onto a *Kirah*, on the other hand, was only prohibited unless some action were performed to mitigate the likelihood of "stoking." Therefore, *Shehiyah* and *chazarah* onto a heating device for which "stoking" does not apply should certainly be permitted.

II

More direct proof that where "stoking" is inapplicable the prohibitions of *Shehiyah* and *chazarah* do not apply, is provided by the Talmudic discussion of the oven sealed with clay. The Talmud differentiates between the permissible *Shehiyah* of the meat of a baby lamb and the prohibited *Shehiyah* of the meat of a ram. Among the differentiations is that the tender meat of a baby lamb is much more quickly cooked than the tough meat of a ram. As a result, the tender meat is generally cooked in an oven whose door is sealed with clay to prevent the fire from flaring up as a result of a gust of wind, and thereby burning the tender meat. The Talmud then questions whether the major lenient factor is the tenderness of the meat, which obviates the likelihood of stoking the coals, since that could burn the meat; or whether the major lenient factor is the sealing of the oven with clay, which renders stoking impossible without going through the bother of breaking the clay seal. The question remained unanswered.[52]

The *Shulchan Arukh*[53] and the *RaMA*[54] derive somewhat conflicting

Halakhic rulings from this discussion. Both concur, however, on the permissibility of *Shehiyah* in an oven sealed with clay for any meat. The *Magen Avraham* bases this permission on the fact that the oven "is not ready to be stoked, because it is sealed."[55]

But the seal can be broken with ease, and the coals can easily be stoked. Nevertheless, the small likelihood of stoking under these circumstances is not great enough to require a Rabbinic prohibition. Accordingly, a rabbinic prohibition should certainly not be required for circumstances in which stoking is impossible. Therefore, *Shehiyah* in an oven for which "stoking" is impossible should be permitted.

The above proof related only to *Shehiyah* and not to *chazarah*, which is not explicitly discussed for an oven sealed with clay. The ruling for *chazarah*, however, can be derived from the ruling for *Hatmanah* in an oven sealed with clay, which is discussed in the Halakhic literature. *Hatmanah*, as mentioned in chapter two, refers to the prohibition of surrounding a pot of food before Shabbat in any heat generating substance. Since *Hatmanah* applies to all heat generating substances, whereas *chazarah* applies only to fire, *Hatmanah* is usually considered a more stringent prohibition than *chazarah*. Thus, if it can be shown that *Hatmanah* in the coals of an oven sealed with clay is permitted, then *chazarah* into an oven sealed with clay should also be permitted.

The *RaMA* permits *Hatmanah* in an oven sealed with clay.[56] His contemporary, the *MaHaRShaL*, disputes this ruling. In his view, since *Hatmanah* is prohibited even in substances for which "stoking" is inapplicable (such as pitch), inapplicability of "stoking" is insufficient reason for permission. The sealed oven could be the Halakhic equivalent of pitch, he concludes, and *Hatmanah* in it should be prohibited.[57]

Even the *MaHaRShaL*, however, could agree that *chazarah*, as opposed to *Hatmanah*, is permitted in an oven sealed with clay. The reason he uses for prohibiting *Hatmanah* in an oven sealed with clay, i.e. that *Hatmanah* is prohibited even in substance for which "stoking" is inapplicable, does not apply to *chazarah*. Accordingly, he too, could permit *chazarah* into an oven sealed with clay.

Furthermore, the *Mishnah B'rurah* cites the long-standing ruling of the *Or Zarua* (a late Rishon) that permits *Hatmanah* in an oven sealed with clay, as an authorative precedent.[58] In his *Sha'ar HaZiyun,* the *Mishnah B'rurah* asserts that had the prohibitors of *Hatmanah* in an oven sealed with clay (such as the *MaHaRShaL*) been aware of the ruling of the *Or Zarua,* they too would have ruled leniently.[59]

The *Chazon Ish* a twentieth century Halakhic authority, contests his conclusion, maintaining that the *Or Zarua* used *"Hatmanah"* in its literal sense — "hiding away food" — rather than in the classic sense. According to him, such "hiding away" is the Halakhic equivalent of *Shehiyah,* which is permitted if the oven is sealed with clay.[60] Thus, the *MaHaRShaL* could still prohibit *Hatmanah* in an oven sealed with clay.

Despite this conclusion of the *Chazon Ish,* however, *chazarah* into an oven sealed with clay seems permissible. The *Mishnah B'rurah* clearly refers to classic *Hatmanah*, and the *RaMA* also seems to refer to classic *Hatmanah*. By implication, they would permit *chazarah* as well. The *MaHaRShaL* certainly understood the *RaMA* as referring to classic *Hatmanah*, and he therefore prohibited *Hatmanah* in an oven sealed with clay. It was shown, however, that even he could permit *chazarah* into an oven sealed with clay. Thus, the views of these authorities give weight to the conclusion that *chazarah* into an oven sealed with clay is permitted.

If *chazarah* into an oven sealed with clay is permitted, however, then why is it not discussed in the Halakhic literature? Quite simply, because *chazarah* — re-placing — into an oven literally sealed with clay is physically impossible. On the other hand, once the clay is removed, and *chazarah* is physically possible, it is no longer permitted. Nevertheless, the basic principle, that when "stoking" is inapplicable *Chazarah* is permitted, can be derived from this discussion. Accordingly, if the equivalent of "stoking" does not apply to a modern heating device, *chazarah* and *Shehiyah* on that device should be permitted.

Chapter 5
Modern Food-Warming Devices on Shabbat

I. General

Before applying the conclusions of the previous four chapters to modern food warming devices, it is necessary to determine how, if at all, "stoking" applies to modern food warming devices. It has been demonstrated that *Shehiyah* and *chazarah* are prohibited only when "stoking" is likely. Accordingly, if it could be shown that "stoking" (or its equivalent) is unlikely in a modern food warming device, then *Shehiyah* and *chazarah* should be permitted on that device.

"Stoking" is necessary when using a *Kirah*, due to the nature of a coal fire. A coal fire generates heat that decreases with time. Stoking the coals improves their combustibility by bringing more oxygen to the fire. When uncooked food is left on a *Kirah* before Shabbat (*Shehiyah*) stoking could be anticipated to increase the heat of the fire and to ensure that the food is edible for the evening meal. As a result, *Shehiyah* is prohibited, unless there is some indication (sweeping the coals or covering them with ash) that further heat is not desired. Similarly, the very act of re-placing food (*chazarah*) onto a *Kirah* indicates that further heat is desired. Accordingly, without some counter-indication, stoking could be anticipated, and, therefore, *chazarah* is prohibited.

On the other hand, modern heating devices are set at some predetermined level that generally remains constant until changed. This being the case, it is never necessary to raise the temperature to counter a natural decrease in temperature, as is the case with coal fires. Accordingly, the whole issue of "stoking" seems far less relevant for modern heat than for coal-fires, and *Shehiyah* and *chazarah* should be permitted for modern food-warming devices.

Nevertheless, if "stoking the coals" is interpreted loosely as "increasing the heat," then "stoking" is relevant for modern heat. If, as *Rabeinu Tam* says (cited in Chapter 2) the very act of *chazarah* indicates a desire for further heat, then increasing the heat is likely for a modern device as well. Accordingly, the prohibition of *chazarah*, and possibly *Shehiyah* as well, could apply to modern food-warming devices.

Yet, if increasing the heat level is analagous to stoking the coals, then lowering the heat setting before Shabbat should be analagous to covering the coals with ash. Lowering the heat setting indicates that further heat is not desired, thereby mitigating the likelihood of "stoking" — increasing — the fire. Accordingly, *Shehiyah* and *chazarah* onto modern food warming devices should be permitted when the heat setting is lowered before Shabbat.

This analogy is, perhaps, less than perfect. When coals are covered with ash (and certainly when they are swept), there is an observable difference in the coals to indicate that no further heat is desired. On the other hand, when the heat level is turned down, there is no observable difference in the fire to indicate that no further heat is desired. Perhaps it is this observable difference that renders *Shehiyah* and *chazarah* permissible?

Nevertheless, the ruling for covered coals that subsequently re-ignite, discussed in the appendix to chapter 2, implies that *Shehiyah* and *chazarah* can be permitted even without any observable difference in the coals. It was indicated that the original action of covering the coals with ash is sufficient indication that no further heat is desired, and that *Shehiyah* and *chazarah* are permitted, regardless of whether or not the coals subsequently burst into flames.

Similarly, the original lowering of the heat level should be sufficient indication that no further heat is desired. Accordingly, *Shehiyah* and *chazarah* should be permitted despite the lack of an observable difference in the fire.

Rabbi Feinstein of New York, one of the leading Halakhic authorities of today, rejects this conclusion, asserting that there is an observable difference in coals covered with ash — even after they re-ignite.[61] If this is so, then lowering the heat level, which makes no observable difference in the fire, would not be analagous to covering the coals with ash. Accordingly, *Shehiyah* and *chazarah* would still be prohibited.

Even if this conclusion is accepted, *Shehiyah* and *chazarah* could perhaps be permitted on modern food-warming devices set to the maxiumum heat level. Under those circumstances, "stoking the coals" — increasing the heat level — is impossible. Since the equivalent of "stoking" is impossible, there is no reason to prohibit *Shehiyah* and *chazarah* when the heat is set at the maximum level.

Or is there? The *Beit Yosef* was cited in Chapter 4 as prohibiting reading by candlelight on Shabbat, despite the fact that the original prohibition of reading was for light that could be tipped. It was explained that although candles are generally not tipped, their wicks are sometimes trimmed, which could extinguish part of the flame. It was further explained that the *Beit Yosef* prohibits an action for which the stated reason for prohibition does not apply, to prevent the likelihood of transgression of another prohibition.

Accordingly, although "stoking the coals" does not apply to a modern food-warming device set to its maximum temperature, *Shehiyah* and *chazarah* could be prohibited nonetheless, to prevent the likelihood of extinguishing the fire (another prohibition).

According to this view, however, *Shehiyah* and *chazarah* on a *Kirah* should also be problematic. Covering the coals with ash mitigates the likelihood of "stoking," but not the likelihood of further covering with ash and extinguishing the coals. Certainly when the coals re-ignite, the likelihood of extinction is great enough to warrant prohibition by this view. *Shehiyah* of tender meat, such as baby lamb, which, as discussed in chapter 4, is easily burnt, should also be prohibited. If not, there is the likelihood of extinguishing the fire to prevent burning the fully cooked tender meat.

From the fact that in these examples *Shehiyah* and *chazarah* are not prohibited, the *Chasdei Avot* concludes that preventing the likelihood of extinction is insufficient cause for prohibition.[62] This view is supported by Rabbi Frank, the late Chief Rabbi of Jerusalem[63] and by Rabbi Yosef, the previous Sephardic Chief Rabbi of Israel. Rabbi Yosef discusses why the likelihood of extinction is insufficient cause for prohibition. One of these reasons, is that the difficulty of extinguishing a coal fire obviates the necessity for a prohibition that prevents the likelihood of extinction. Although this reason does not apply to modern devices, in which a simple turn of a knob extinguishes the fire, Rabbi Yosef nevertheless concludes that no new prohibitions would apply to modern heating devices. In his view, a prohibition can only be based upon preventive measures that have a Talmudic basis. Any preventive measure without Talmudic basis, such as preventing the likelihood of extinction, is insufficient cause for prohibition.[64]

Rabbi Feinstein of New York, however, prohibits *chazarah* on modern food-warming devices to prevent extinction unless some indication in the fire itself serves as a reminder not to extinguish.[65] Even according to this view, however, *Shehiyah* and *chazarah* on modern food-warming devices could be permitted under circumstances derived from the "oven sealed with clay" (See chapter 4 Part II). Covering the control knobs of a modern food-warming device with tape should be analagous to "sealing" an oven with clay. In either case, heat can be increased - "stoking" — only after an inconvenient process, which serves as a reminder that it is Shabbat. In addition, when the controls are covered with tape, extinction becomes an inconvenient process as well, thereby obviating any prohibition based upon extinction.

Accordingly, *Shehiyah* and *chazarah* on a modern food-warming device whose controls are covered with tape should have the same ruling as *Shehiyah* and *chazarah* on an oven sealed with clay. Since *Shehiyah* in an oven sealed with clay is permitted, it should be permitted for a modern food-warming device whose controls are covered with tape as well. The ruling for *chazarah*, however, is unclear. The *Chazon Ish* prohibits *chazarah* in an oven "sealed with clay" saying "...we find no permission for placing on Shabbat."[66] Nevertheless, it was shown in chapter 4 that most other authorities could permit *chazarah* in an oven "sealed" with clay. Even according to the *Chazon Ish*, removing the knobs could make *chazarah* permissible, since it is then all but impossible to change the heat level.

These conclusions are dependent upon one of the central theses of this section: That the reason *chazarah* is prohibited is to prevent the likelihood of "stoking." The appendix to chapter two supported this thesis at great length. Nevertheless, Rabbi Frank, the late Chief Rabbi of Jerusalem, Rabbi Feinstein of New York and other major Halakhic authorities base the prohibition of *chazarah* on the fact that it "appears as cooking." Accordingly, they prohibit *chazarah* on modern stoves, even after removing the control knobs, since it still "appears as cooking."[67]

Furthermore, it has become customary to cover the fire of gas and electric stoves on Shabbat with tin or asbestos.[67a] Widely accepted customs such as these, assume Halakhic validity.[68] Thus, even if from a theoretical standpoint *Shehiyah* and *chazarah* can be permitted over an open fire under the circumstances described above, from a practical Halakhic viewpoint the permission applies only when the fire is covered with tin or asbestos. When covering "the fire" is inapplicable, however, as in the case of a warming bath, the control knob may be removed, and *Shehiyah* and *chazarah* permitted.

As explained in chapter 3, the permission for *chazarah* applies only when the conditions for *chazarah* are fulfilled. These conditions are:
1. The food is still hot,
2. The intention to re-place is present at the time of removal,
3. The food should not be put down, or at least not put down on the floor,
4. The food should be fully cooked.

When these conditions are fulfilled, *chazarah* is permitted onto a tin or asbestos covered fire (or, when that is impossible, onto a device whose control knob is removed). When these conditions are not fulfilled, the act of re-placing could not be defined as *chazarah*, because it appears to be a new placement which is prohibited because it "appears as cooking."

Anything that "appears as cooking" is prohibited on Shabbat. As a result, if the conditions for *chazarah* are not fulfilled, re-placing (and certainly placing) food on Shabbat is prohibited, even if the control knobs are removed and the fire covered with tin or asbestos. The only permitted Shabbat placement even onto a stove covered with tin or asbestos is re-placing food that had previously been on the fire if the conditions for *chazarah* are fulfilled. Any other Shabbat placement onto a cooking area is prohibited.

On the other hand, it could perhaps be permitted to place food onto a device used for heat maintenance only, provided that there is just one setting. Since there is just one setting, "stoking" is impossible. It does not "appear as cooking" either, because the temperature used for those devices are too low for cooking. As such, fully cooked cold dry food (but *not* liquids) could be warmed up on devices such as a non-adjustable hot-plate.[69]

Needless to say, there are no conditions that would permit placing uncooked food, or even fully cooked cold liquids, on Shabbat onto an area that can cook food. Such placement can transgress the Torah prohibition of *Bishul* when the food is heated to a given temperature and transgresses a Rabbinic prohibition even if removed before that temperature is reached. This prohibition applies equally to all heat sources.

In summation: Because of the custom to cover the fire with tin or asbestos, *Shehiyah* on modern stoves could always be permitted only when the fire is covered. *Chazarah* is also permitted under those circumstances, but only if the conditions for *chazarah* are fulfilled. Any other Shabbat placement onto a cooking area can either transgress the Torah prohibition of *Bishul* if the food involved is uncooked or is a cold liquid, or transgress the Rabbinic prohibition of *mechaze Ki-mevashel* for all other food.

II. *Transferral to a New Vessel*

This permission for *chazarah* applies to re-placing the same vessel that was removed. Many institutions that cook large quantities, transfer food cooked on the stove into the pots of a heat maintenance device. Is this permissible on Shabbat? Does the transfer to a new vessel remove the placement from the category of *chazarah* even if all the conditions for *chazarah* are fulfilled?

This question, as mentioned in Chapter 3, was asked by the Talmud and no answer was given. *Rabeinu Chananel*, a tenth century predecessor of the Rishonim era, rules that all unanswered Talmudic questions of this type are ruled prohibitively (*Teiku D'issura Le'Chumra*)[70] The *ROsh*, as well as his son the *Tur*, concur with this ruling.[71] On the other hand, the *RaMBaM* omits this case when he enummerates those cases for which *chazarah* is prohibited.[72] This omission in that comprehensive encyclopedic work, is considered by *Rabbi Yosef Karo*, in his commentary on the *Tur, Beit Yosef,* evidence that the *RaMBaM* permits such *chazarah*.[73] Accordingly, *Rabbi Karo* also omits this prohibition from his *Shulchan Arukh*. Although the *RaMA* does not comment on this omission, the *Magen Avraham* indicates that he nevertheless prohibits *chazarah* under those circumstances.[74] The *Shulchan Arukh HaRav* also rules prohibitively,[75] whereas the *Mishnah B'rurah*, in his *Sha'ar Ha'Tziyun*, seems to rule leniently.[76]

Thus, the unsolved Talmudic question remains unsolved in our times as well. *Rabeinu Chanan'el*, the *ROsh, Tur, RaMA* according to the *Magen Avraham*, and the *Shulchan Arukh HaRav* all rule prohibitively. On the other hand, the *RaMBaM, Shulchan Arukh,* and the *Mishnah B'rurah* in his *Sha'ar HaTziyun* rule leniently. Accordingly, it is difficult to permit *chazarah* of food transferred to a second vessel.

Nevertheless, carefully analyzing how the commentaries understood the Talmudic question, indicates a permitted method for transferring into pots of heat-maintaining devices on Shabbat. Many of the Rishonim ask the question cited in chapter 3: Why is *Hatmanah* more lenient and *chazarah* more stringent when transferring to another vessel, despite the fact that *Hatmanah* is generally considered the more stringent prohibition? Many answers were given, Rabeinu Tam, the Rosh, and the *RaN* give various differentiations between the nature of *Hatmanah* and the nature of *chazarah*.[77] From the fact that they, as well as *RaShI*,[77a] the *RaShBa*[77b] and the *Meiri*[77c] do not differentiate between the circumstances for which *Hatmanah* is permitted and for which *chazarah* is questionable, it can be inferred that the circumstances are similar.[78] Since the Talmud explicitly states that the second vessel in the case of *Hatmanah* is colder than the first, it can be assumed that in the case of *chazarah* the second vessel is also colder than the first. If, however, the second vessel is not colder than the first, such *chazarah* could be permitted.

Proof that when the second vessel is not colder than the first, *chazarah* is permitted, can be brought from the commentaries of the *Shulchan Arukh*. The *Shulchan Arukh* prohibits adding hot water to hot food over the fire.[79] The *TaZ* and the *Magen Avraham* discuss the circumstances for which it is permitted to add water and the circumstances for which it is prohibited.[80] Despite the fact that adding water is, in effect, *chazarah* in a second vessel, it is clear from their discussion that the only factor involved is the Torah prohibition of *Bishul*. Presumably, the pouring into the second vessel is not an issue because the second vessel is also hot.

Thus, it is permitted to transfer hot food into pots of a heat maintaining device provided that the pots are also hot. The fact that *chazarah* usually refers to returning to the same heating unit, whereas here, two units are involved, does not affect this permission. The *RaMBaM* permits *chazarah* onto a second *Kirah*[81] and the *Magen Avraham* indicates that the *RaMA* agrees with this ruling and that that is the Halakhah.[82] Thus, transfer to a heat maintaining device should be permitted.

One other problem must be solved, however. Stirring hot food (*Meigiss*) over a fire is Rabbinically prohibited as a form of cooking. This prohibition applies even when the food is fully cooked and the fire covered. As a result, it is prohibited to pour food into a pot on the fire, or to remove food with a spoon or ladle from a pot on the fire, since either of these actions could stir the food.[83]

Thus, since the electric heat of the heat maintenance device can be considered fire (see Section IV), the food should be transferred only if both the cooking pot and the heat maintaining pot are not on their sources of heat. If they are not on their sources of heat, then the problem of *chazarah* arises when returning the pots to their respective heat sources, unless the conditions of *chazarah* are fulfilled. Since one of these conditions is that the pot should not be put down, the food should be gently transferred with one person holding the large cooking pot and another holding the heat-maintaining pot. Both pots could then be re-placed onto their sources of heat.

This solution, however, is generally impractical, even when several people are available for help. An alternate solution, where necessary, is to place the large pot onto a stool or other temporary resting place, maintaining physical contact if possible. Although the *RaMA* prohibits *chazarah* whenever the pot is put down, the *Mishnah B'rurah* cites many sources who permit *chazarah* if the pot is put down onto a temporary resting place.[84] Furthermore, the *RaMA* himself defines *chazarah* as the *RaN* does: Re-placing on Shabbat food that was removed before Shabbat.[85] Food removed on Shabbat, according to this view, does not cancel the original *Shehiyah*, does not "appear as cooking," and may be re-placed even if the conditions for *chazarah* are not fulfilled. Although the *RaMA* concludes that it is preferable not to rely on this ruling,[86] nevertheless, combined with the lenient ruling of the *Mishnah B'rurah*, such *chazarah* should be permitted.

To summarize the permitted method of transferring from a cooking pot on a stove to the pots of a heat maintaining device without transgressing the prohibitions of *Meigiss*, or of *chazarah*: The pots and ladle should be left on a covered fire before Shabbat. Whenever possible both pots should be held away from their respective heat sources while the food is gently transferred into the heat maintaining pot. When this method is impractical, the cooking pot can be placed on a stool, or other temporary resting place, physical contact should be maintained if possible, and the food can be gently transferred. In either case, both pots may be re-placed on their respective heat sources.

III. Ovens

The entire section, thus far, dealt with *chazarah onto* a *Kirah* or *onto* a modern heating device. The top of a *Kirah* was used for cooking or heat maintenance, whereas the inside of a *Kirah* was used for cooking only. Therefore, *chazarah* into the inside of a *Kirah* "appears as cooking" more than *chazarah* onto the top of a *Kirah* does. Accordingly, the *Shulchan Arukh* prohibits all *chazarah* into the inside of a *Kirah*.[87] At first glance, the stoves of today are analagous to the top of a *Kirah*, whereas the ovens of today are analogous to the inside of a *Kirah*. If that is so, then *chazarah* into a modern oven should be prohibited. However, the *Magen Avraham*, *Shulchan Arukh HaRav*, *Arukh HaShulchan*, and *Mishnah B'rurah* all concur with the ruling of the *Shiltei Giborim*, a Rishon, who says "Our *Kirahs* that are simple, have the same lenient ruling for the top and the inside."[88] The *Arukh HaShulchan*, a turn of the century codification of the *Shulchan Arukh* and the subsequent commentaries, explains that "simple" refers to the fact that food is always placed on the inside, since there is no top on which to place food. Accordingly, the same surface is, in effect, the "top" and the "inside". Therefore, *chazarah* into the inside of "our *Kirahs*" is permitted.[89]

On the one hand, only the inside of a modern oven is used for cooking. Perhaps the logic of the *Arukh HaShulchan* should, therefore, permit *chazarah* into a modern oven on Shabbat. On the other hand, the temperatures inside an oven are hotter than the temperature on top of a stove. As a result, the oven is generally reserved for cooking, while rewarming is generally done on the stove top. Perhaps, therefore, our ovens, unlike "our *Kirahs*" mentioned above, are analagous to the inside of a *Kirah* for which *chazarah* is prohibited.

Unlike the ruling for transferring from one vessel to another discussed above, there is insufficient indication of permission for this case to combine with the *RaN*'s lenient definition of *chazarah*. Accordingly, *chazarah* into the inside of an oven should be prohibited even for food removed on Shabbat.[90] Nevertheless, due to the unclear nature of the prohibition, *chazarah* should be permitted for hospitals and those in other circumstances of duress, especially when the food was removed from the fire on Shabbat (See Section V for the problem of thermostatic control).

IV. *Steam Heat*

Among the modern food warming devices, those based upon steam heat merit a discussion of their own, due to the fact that less Halakhic problems are generally involved. A steam kitchen is an example of a steam heater. A boiler, in a room generally below the kitchen, boils water into steam that is fed into pipes leading to a heating system in the kitchen. The entry of the steam is controlled by opening and closing a spigot. The entire system is closed, so that the steam is constantly recycled. The heat of the steam can either cook the food or maintain its heat, depending upon how much steam is allowed to enter.

Cooking food in steam heat transgresses the prohibition of *Bishul* just as if it were cooked on the fire. Similarly, the prohibition of *mechaze Ki-mevashel* is not mitigated in a steam system. *Shehiyah* and *chazarah*, however, are less stringent in a steam system.

The problem of "stoking" does not apply to steam systems. First of all, the system is generally designed so that the adjustment of the flame is impossible. Second of all, a person would remember that it is Shabbat during the time necessary to reach the boiler room, just as he would remember in the time necessary to remove a clay seal from an oven (See chapter 4). Thirdly, even if opening the spigot of the steam is compared to "stoking the coals" no prohibition is needed to prevent opening the spigot. Although many authorities prohibit opening and closing the spigot because of the possible effect it can have on the thermostatically controlled boiler,[91] others permit opening the spigot.[92]

In their view, since there is no way of knowing whether the fire in the boiler is on or off at the time of action, the doubtful re-ignition of the fire by the thermostat is insufficient reason for prohibition. Even those who prohibit turning the spigot, consider the prohibition Rabbinic, so that it is inappropriate to institute a new prohibition to prevent transgression. Thus, although the Halakhah is that opening (or closing) the spigot should in fact be prohibited, *Shehiyah* and *chazarah* on such systems need not be prohibited to prevent its occurrence.

Other problems also do not apply. The problem of extinction does not apply for the same three reasons that "stoking" does not apply. The possible *Bishul* of any cold water that enters the system to replace evaporated steam, is no different than the possible re-ignition of the fire, and it too, is no reason for prohibition.

In summation: Opening and closing the faucets of a steam system can transgress a Rabbinic prohibition. Nevertheless, *Shehiyah* and *chazarah* (but *not Bishul* or *mechaze Ki-mevashel*) are permitted in such systems. Certainly, if the conditions enumerated for the other modern heating devices are followed, its use is preferable to those devices.

Chapter 2 — Appendix
Proof that the Prohibition of *Chazarah* is Based upon "Stoking"

The general term "placement" was used throughout chapter two, rather than the more specific terms *Shehiyah* and *chazarah*. Implicit in the use of that term here is the assumption that both *Shehiyah* and *chazarah* are prohibited to prevent the likelihood of "stoking" the coals. This assumption has one flaw. *Chazarah* is prohibited by those who follow the ruling of Chananiah, under certain circumstances in which *Shehiyah* is permitted, as explained in chapter two. This could indicate a different prohibitory factor for *chazarah* than for *Shehiyah*. The purpose of this appendix is to prove that the prohibitory factor for *chazarah* onto a *Kirah* whose coals are neither swept nor covered with ash is in fact to prevent the likelihood of stoking the coals.

The basic question, why *chazarah* is prohibited under certain circumstances in which *Shehiyah* is permitted, is answered by *Rabeinu Tam,* a grandson of *RaShI* and a major author of *Tosfot,* in his *Sefer HaYashar*:

"... Since he places the food [on Shabbat or soon before Shabbat] on or in it [the *Kirah*], he clearly indicates his thoughts that it requires heating. Thus, we fear that he may stoke [to increase the heat and hasten the heating process]. Indications such as sweeping or covering with ash are therefore required [as reminders]."[93]

This explains why *Rabeinu Tam* permits, in accordance with the view of Chananiah, *Shehiyah* of food cooked to the level of *Ma'akhal Ben Derusai,* without sweeping or covering with ash, and yet prohibits *chazarah* of the same food, unless the coals are swept or covered. When *Ma'akhal Ben Derusai* food is left on the *Kirah* before Shabbat, it is assumed that there is no purpose in stoking the coals, since the food would be edible in either case for the night meal. The very action of re-placing cooked food on a fire, even before Shabbat, however, clearly indicates that extra heat is desired, thereby increasing the likelihood of stoking the coals. This likelihood is mitigated only by a counteraction, such as sweeping the coals or covering them with ash, to indicate that additional heat is not desired.

The *RI*, a major authority of the *Tosfot* school one generation after *Rabeinu Tam*, disagrees with *Rabbeinu Tam*. In his view, re-placing a pot before Shabbat could only be considered *chazarah* if re-placed at a time when the pot could no longer boil before the onset of Shabbat. Nevertheless, he seems to agree that the reason for prohibition is to prevent the likelihood of "stoking."[94] Indeed, many other Rishonim seem to agree with the reason explicitly given by the *Ba'al HaMa'or:* "A preventive measure against the likelihood of stoking the coals."[95]

RaShI however, explains that *chazarah* is prohibited because it "appears as cooking" (*mechaze Ki-mevashel*).[96] As indicated in chapter one, anything prohibited because of *mechaze Ki-mevashel* is prohibited for any cooking device regardless of the applicability of "stoking." Accordingly, a device in which "stoking" is inapplicable could seemingly illustrate the practical difference between the reasons for prohibiting *chazarah*. If the reason is to prevent the likelihood of "stoking," then the prohibition seems unnecessary for a device in which "stoking" is inapplicable. On the other hand, if the reason is because of *mechaze Ki-mevashel*, then the prohibition should apply equally to all devices in which *Bishul* can occur.

There is another practical difference between the two reasons. A prohibition based upon *mechaze Ki-mevashel* could only be prohibited at a time in which *Bishul* itself is prohibited. Since *Bishul* is not prohibited until the onset of Shabbat, anything "appearing as cooking" could not be prohibited until the onset of Shabbat. By extension, all views that prohibit *chazarah* before Shabbat (*Rabbeinu Tam*[97] *RI*,[98] *Rosh*[99]) cannot base the prohibition on *mechaze Ki-mevashel*.

At any rate, this view, that *chazarah* is prohibited because of *mechaze Ki-mevashel*, has been introduced here as the view of *Rashi*. Yet, it is by no means clear that *Rashi* bases the Halakhic prohibition of *chazarah* on *mechaze Ki-mevashel*. *Rashi*'s commentary is a phrase by phrase elucidation of the Talmudic discussion, regardless of the subsequent Halakhic conclusion. His explanation of the prohibition of *chazarah* appears under the heading ["Beit Shamai says... but] not replace." Beit Shamai prohibits *chazarah* even after sweeping the coals or covering them with ash. Accordingly, the prohibition could not be based on the likelihood of "stoking," which is mitigated by those actions. *Rashi* concludes, therefore, that the prohibition of Beit Shamai must be based upon *mechaze Ki-mevashel*. *Rashi* does not comment on the Halakhically accepted view of Beit Hillel, that *chazarah* is prohibited "until he sweeps or covers with ash." However, the *MaHaRaM* of Lublin, a commentary on *Rashi* and *Tosfot* who lived in the early Acharonim era, asserts that *Rashi* would agree that this prohibition is to prevent the likelihood of "stoking."[100]

The *Ran*'s commentary to the codification of the *RIF*, however, was primarily concerned with the Halakhah. When explaining the Talmudic interpretation of "placing" (*yiten*) as "replacing" (*chazarah*) he bases the prohibition for *chazarah* on *mechaze Ki-mevashel*. Otherwise, maintains the *Ran, chazarah* should have the same ruling as *Shehiyah*. If *Shehiyah* of *ma'akhal Ben Derusai* food is permitted without sweeping the coals or covering them with ash, whereas *chazarah* of such food is not, then the reason for prohibiting *chazarah* must be different from the reason for prohibiting *Shehiyah*. This reason, concludes the *RaN,* is that *chazarah* is *mechaze Ki-mevashel*.[101]

Conversely, if the Mishnaic "placed" (*yiten*) refers to *Shehiyah*, thereby indicating that *Shehiyah* is prohibited for *ma'akhal Ben Derusai* as well, then *Shehiyah* and *chazarah* have the same ruling. If *Shehiyah* and *chazarah* have the same ruling, then the reason for the two can be the same, and even the *RaN* could base the prohibitions on "stoking." As previously indicated, however, the (Ashkenazi) Halakhic view is that the Mishnaic "placed" refers to *chazarah*. Accordingly, the *RaN* bases the prohibition on *mechaze Ki-mevashel*.

The obvious question is why, according to this view, is *chazarah* permitted if the coals are swept or covered with ash? The answer must be that when coals are swept or covered with ash, a difference is apparent in the *Kirah*. This difference removes the appearance of cooking, and consequently *chazarah* is permitted.

Yet, the Talmud rules that "placing" over coals that had been covered with ash is permitted even after the coals re-ignite.[102] If *chazarah* is prohibited to prevent the likelihood of "stoking", then, as mentioned in chapter two, the covering with ash indicated that no further heat is desired, regardless of subsequent development. Accordingly, *chazarah* can be permitted. If, however, *chazarah* is prohibited because it "appears as cooking," "placing" after the coals re-ignite would "appear as cooking" and should be prohibited, contrary to the Talmudic ruling.

One possible solution to this question on the *RaN* is to interpret the "placed" of this Mishnaic ruling as referring to *Shehiyah*. Accordingly, *Shehiyah*, based upon the likelihood of "stoking," is permitted over coals that re-burst into flame. *Chazarah*, on the other hand, based upon the "appearance of cooking," can be prohibited over such coals, in accordance with the ruling of the *RaN*.

This solution, however, contradicts the implication of the Talmudic discussion on the Mishnah of *Kirah*. Implicit in this discussion is that whereas the rulings for *Shehiyah* change dependent upon whether or not "placed" refers to *Shehiyah*, the rulings for *chazarah* do not. This is so, because *chazarah* is permitted by Beit Hillel (the Halakhic view) in both interpretations, and no differentiations are made by the Talmudic rulings concerning *chazarah*, regardless of the interpretation accepted. It is, therefore, difficult to postulate a difference concerning *chazarah* over covered coals that re-ignite.

Furthermore, the Halakhic conclusion seems to be that *chazarah* is permitted over covered coals that re-ignite. This is supported by Rishonim such as the *RaMBaN* and *RITVA,*, who explicitly permit *chazarah* under such circumstances[103] and by the *RaN* himself who considers such coals as if they were "completely covered."[104] The *Magen Avraham* also concludes that coals are considered "covered with ash" regardless of whether or not they subsequently re-ignite.[105]

To further develop the question on the *RaN*, this ruling of the *Magen Avraham* must be analyzed. This ruling comments on the portion of the *Shulchan Arukh* that explains the view that "placed" refers to *Shehiyah*. The *Magen Avraham*, among many other commentaries of the *Shulchan Arukh*, indicates when a specific ruling derived from the first interpretation, does not apply to the Halakhically accepted second interpretation.[106] Since the *Magen Avraham* makes no such indications for his ruling for covered coals, it seems to apply equally to both interpretations.

The *Mishnah B'rurah*, cites this ruling of the *Magen Avraham* and considers it Halakhically binding.[107] His footnotes, the *Sha'ar Ha'Ziyun*, bases the ruling on the above-cited rulings of the *RaMBaN*, *RITVA* and *RaN* who conclude, in his paraphrase, "that it is equivalent to covering with ash in all respects."[108] This phrase, "in all respects," seemingly indicates that *chazarah* is permitted over coals that subsequently burst into flame. Since the Halakha seems to be that *chazarah* is permitted over such coals, it is no longer possible to explain that this ruling applies only if the Mishnaic "placed" applies to *Shehiyah*, which is not the Halakhically accepted view. Thus, the view of the *RaN* seems rejected by the Halakhah.

An alternate possibility in answering the question on the *RaN*, is to postulate that whereas the *RaN* prohibits *chazarah* because it "appears as cooking," no new rulings need result. Accordingly, whether "placing" in the Mishnah of *Kirah* refers to *Shehiyah*, and the prohibitory factor for *chazarah* is "stoking," or whether "placing" refers to *chazarah*, and the prohibitory factor for *chazarah* is "appearing as cooking," all the subrulings are the same. Thus, a subruling (such as *chazarah* over coals that re-ignite) that applies when "placing" refers to *Shehiyah*, can apply even if "placing" is understood as referring to *chazarah*. If that is so, then applying *chazarah* to any new case depends upon the applicability of "stoking", not whether or not it "appears as cooking."

Needless to say, such a "solution" appears illogical since it postulates that a prohibition based upon "appearing as cooking" is permitted when "stoking" does not apply. The only alternative, however, is the previously discussed solution which postulates that the *RaN* applies the ruling for covered coals that re-ignite only to the view that "placed" refers to *Shehiyah*. Since the accepted Halakhic view is both that "placed" refers to *chazarah* and that *chazarah* is permitted over covered coals that re-ignite, the Halakhah apparently rejects that alternative. In either case, however, the Halakhic conclusion appears to be that *chazarah* is permitted when stoking does not apply.

The *Mishnah B'rurah* also seems to indicate that there is no practical Halakhic difference between basing *chazarah* on "stoking" or on "appearing as cooking." In one ruling he bases the prohibition on preventing the possibility of stoking.¹⁰⁹ Elsewhere, however, he writes, "...re-placing on Shabbat appears as cooking if they [the coals] are not swept.¹¹⁰" In his *Sha'ar HaZiyun* he cites the *RaN* as the source for this latter ruling, and continues: "and in the *Sefer Hayashar* [of *Rabeinu Tam*] it says, sweeping is required because when he removes it [the pot] from the fire it cools off a bit, and we fear that he may stoke as he re-places."¹¹¹

The fact that both sources are cited with no differentiation made between them, could indicate that the *Mishnah B'rurah* felt that there was no practical Halakhic difference between them. Since "stoking" has been shown to be the main prohibitory factor, presumably the *Mishnah B'rurah* could also permit *chazarah* whenever "stoking" does not apply. Indeed, it has been shown that he does permit *chazarah* over covered coals that re-ignite, despite the fact that it seemingly "appears as cooking."¹¹²

In summation: most Rishonim base the prohibition of *chazarah* on "stoking the coals." Even *Rashi*, who seems to base the prohibition on "appearing as cooking," can be understood to base the Halakhic prohibition on "stoking the coals." Only the *RaN* bases the Halakhic prohibition on the "appearance of cooking." The difficulty in this view, caused by the ruling that permits *chazarah* over covered coals that re-ignite, was discussed. Two solutions were presented for this difficulty. According to both solutions the only Halakhically relevant factor for *chazarah* is the likelihood of stoking the coals. Thus, *chazarah* as well as *Shehiyah* should be permitted whenever stoking the coals does not apply.

Section I

1. *Rambam,* Laws of Shabbat 9:1 and 9:6
2. *Rashi,* Shabbat 20a s.v. *Ben Derusai*
3. *Rambam,* Laws of Shabbat 9:5; *Ra'avad* Laws of Shabbat 9:5
4. For a fuller discussion see Section IV.
5. TB Shabbat 145b; *Rambam* Laws of Shabbat 9:3; Shulchan Arukh, Orach Chaim 318:4
6. See Chapter 3
7. Shabbat 3:1
8. TB Shabbat 36b
9. *ibid*
10. *op. cit*
11. *Rama,* Shulchan Arukh, Orach Chaim 253:1
12. *Biur Halakha* 253 s.v. *Venahagu*
13. Shulchan Arukh, Orach Chaim 253:2
14. *Rashi* Shabbat 36b s.v. *Ad Sheyigrof*
15. *Tosfot* Shabbat 36b s.v. *Lo Yiten*
16. *Hagahot VeChidushin LeHaREM Hurwitz* Shabbat 36b
17. *Tur,*Orach Chaim 253; *Beit Yosef,* Orach Chaim 253 s.v. *Kirah*; Shulchan Arukh Orach Chaim 253:1
18. *Rambam,* Laws of Shabbat 3:4-6
19. *Chidushei HaRamban,* Shabbat chapter Kirah, s.v. *Ad Sheyigrof*
20. *Chidushei HaRashba,* Shabbat, chapter Kirah, s.v. *Ad Sheyigrof*
21. TJ Shabbat 3:1
22. TB Shabbat 38b
23. TB Shabbat 37a
24. *ibid.*
25. *Chidushei HaRashba, op. cit.*
26. *Magen Avraham,* Orach Chaim 253:3; *Shulchan Arukh Harav* 253:1; *Mishnah B'rurah* 253:14; *Sha'ar Ha'tziyun* 253:17
27. *Hama'or HaKatan,* Shabbat 36b s.v. *Ve'im Tish'al*
28. *Ran Al Harif,* Shabbat 36b s.v. *Ad Sheyigrof*
29. *Tur* Orach Chaim 253; *Bach* Orach Chaim 253; *Magen Avraham* 253:8; *Shulkhan Aruch HaRav* 253:5; *Mishnah B'rurah* Orach Chaim 253:22

30. TB Shabbat 38b
31. *Shulchan Arukh* Orach Chaim 253:2
32. TB Shabbat 38b
33. *Tosfot HaROSH*, Shabbat 38B s.v. *Pinah*
34. *Shulchan Arukh* Orach Chaim 328:1
35. Cf. *Tosfot* TB Beza 30a s.v. *T'nan Ein; Badei Ha'Shulchan* 134:7.2
36. TB Shabbat 11a
37. Tosefta Shabbat 1:6
38. *Hagahot Asheri*, Shabbat 1:27 s.v. *Mesapka*
39. *Beit Yosef*, Orach Chaim 275 s.v. *"Ve'Katav Rabeinu Peretz"*
40. *Bach* Orach Chaim 275 s.v. *Ve'katav*
41. *Magen Avraham*, Orach Chaim 275:3
42. *Taz*, Orach Chaim 275:2
43. *Shulchan Arukh HaRav*, Orach Chaim 275:1; *Kuntres Acharon*, Orach Chaim 275:2
44. *Mishnah B'rurah*, Orach Chaim 275:4
45. *Misgeret HaShulchan*, Lechem Hapanim 80:9
46. *Biur Halakhah*, Orach Chaim 275 s.v. *Le'Or HaNer*
47. *Bach* Orach Chaim 275 s.v. *"Ein Polin"; Magen Avraham* Orach Chaim 275:2; *Taz* Orach Chaim 275:1
48. *Eliyahu Rabah*, Orach Chaim 275:2
49. *Pri Megadim* Eshel Avraham 275:3; *Arukh HaShulchan*, Orach Chaim 275:10
50. *Biur Halakhah*, Orach Chaim 275:1 s.v. *Le'or*
51. See *Chashmal Ba'Halakhah* volume II, for a concise review of the literature concerning reading by the light of electricity, a light for which neither tipping nor trimming is applicable.
52. TB Shabbat 18b
53. *Shulchan Arukh*, Orach Chaim 254:1
54. *RAMA*, Orach Chaim 254:1
55. *Magen Avraham* Orach Chaim 254:5
56. *RAMA*, Orach Chaim 257:8
57. *Shut MaHaRshah*, chapter 60
58. *Mishnah B'rurah*, Orach Chaim 257:47
59. *Sha'ar HaTziyun*, Orach Chaim 257:46
60. *Chazon Ish*, Shabbat Laws 37:20
61. *Igrot Mosheh*, Orach Chaim Volume 4:74 *Bishul* - 30
62. *Chasdei Avot*, cited in *Shut HarTzvi*, Orach Chaim 1:32
63. *Shut HarTzvi*, Orach Chaim 1:132
64. *Yabia Omer*, 1:16

65. *Igrot Mosheh,* Orach Chaim 1:93; Orach Chaim IV:74 *Bishul* — 25
66. *Chazon Ish* Orach Chaim 38:2
67. *Igrot Mosheh,* Orach Chaim IV:74 *Bishul* — 30; *Shut HarTzvi,* Orach Chaim I *"Harerei Sadeh"* 136;
67A. *Igrot Moshe* Orach Chaim I:93 prefers that the knobs be covered as well.
68. *Shulchan Arukh* Yoreah De'ah 214:2; *Pri Chadash,* Orach Chaim 496; *Mateh Efrayim* 610:11; *Beit Yosef,* Yoreh Deah 39
69. *Pri Megadim,* Eshel Avraham 253:36; *L'vushei S'rad,* Orach Chaim 318:8; *Mishnah B'rurah* 318:59. Cf. *Igrot Mosheh* Orach Chaim IV:74 — Bishul 35
70. *Rabeinu Chanan'el* TB Shabbat 38b
71. *Rosh,* TB Shabbat 3:2; *Tur,* Orach Chaim 253
72. *Rambam* Shabbat Laws 3
73. *Beit Yosef,* Orach Chaim 253. s.v. *"Umah Sh'ekatav"*
74. *Magen Avraham,* Orach Chaim 253:20
75. *Shulchan Arukh HaRav* Orach Chaim 253:4
76. *Sha'ar HaTziyun* Orach Chaim 253:16
77. *Tosfot HaRosh,* Shabbat 38b s.v. *"Pinah;" Tosfot* Shabbat 38B s.v. *"Pinah" Ran al Harif* Shabbat 38b
77A. *Rashi,* Shabbat 38b s.v. *"Pinah."*
77B. *Chidushei HaRashba,* Shabbat 38b s.v. *Ha*
77C. *Chidushei HaMe'iri* Shabbat 38b
78. The *Ran* gives a second answer which does differentiate between the circumstances for *Hatmanah* and for *chazarah.*
79. *Shulchan Arukh* Orach Chaim 253:4
80. *Taz,* Orach Chaim 253:17; *Magen Avraham* 253:32
81. *Rambam,* Shabbat laws 3:11
82. *Magen Avraham* 253:23
83. *Rama,* Orach Chaim 318:18; *Mishnah B'rurah* 318:117
84. *Biur Halakhah,* 253:2 s.v. *"V'Da'ato"; Mishnah B'rurah* 253:56
85. *Rama,* Orach Chaim 253:2
86. *ibid.*
87. *Shulchan Arukh,* Orach Chaim 253:2
88. *Magen Avraham* Orach Chaim 253:22; Shulchan Arukh HaRav 253:14; *Mishnah B'rurah,* Orach Chaim 253:58; *Arukh HaShulchan* 253:7.
89. *Arukh HaShulchan, ibid.*
90. Based on the preference of the *Rama* not to rely on this ruling of the *Ran*
91. See Section V:2 especially concerning *Safek Pesik Reisha Le'She'avar.*
92. For more information see *Chimum Mayim B'Shabbat* 7:7.
93. *Sefer HaYashar Le'Rabeinu Tam,* chapter 235

94. *Tosfot* Shabbat 36b s.v. *U'Beit Hillel*
95. *Hama'or HaKatan*, Shabbat chapter 3 s.v. *She'Hisikuha*
96. *Rashi*, Shabbat 36b s.v. *Lo*
97. *op cit.* The Mishnaic words "*until* he sweeps" imply that the placement is at a time when sweeping is permitted. i.e. before Shabbat
98. *op cit.*
99. *Rosh* Shabbat 3:2. At first glance the *Rosh* seems to base the pre-Shabbat prohibition on *Mechaze KiMevashel*. Closer scrutiny indicates that the Rosh is explaining the view of Beit Shamai, and not the Halakhically binding view of Beit Hillel. The Korban Netanel (3:20) explains that what applies to Beit Shamai, when swept, applies to Beit Hillel when not swept. Nevertheless, the Rosh, is referring to fully cooked food, specifically according to Beit Shamai. If the Rosh, a halakhic work, does not explain this point according to Beit Hillel, then apparently he feels that Beit Hillel would not prohibit re-placing fully cooked food before Shabbat, seemingly because the basis for Chazarah is "stoking the coals." On the other hand, if Beit Shamai prohibits replacing before Shabbat, then it is because of a preventive measure based on *Mechaze Ki'mevashel* that applies only to Beit Shamai.
100. *Maharam*, Shabbat chapter 3, s.v. *Dibur Hamatchil Aval*
101. *Ran Al Harif*, chapter 3, s.v. *Iba'aya Lehu,* c.f. *Rabeinu Tam* op. cit.
102. TB Shabbat 37a
103. *Chidushei HaRamban,* Shabbat chapter 3, s.v. *Shma Minah Mitztamek; Chidushei Haritva* Shabbat chapter 3, s.v. *Shma Minah Mitztamek*
104. *Ran al Harif* Shabbat Chapter 3, s.v. *Iba'aya*. Note that in *Chidushei HaRan* s.v. *Shma Mina* he seems to say that Chazarah over coals that reignite is prohibited.
105. *Magen Avraham*, Orach Chaim 253:3
106. e.g. *Magen Avraham* Orach Chaim 253:5 and 253:6
107. *Mishnah B'rurah*, Orach Chaim 253:14
108. *Sha'ar haTziyun*, Orach Chaim 253:17
109. *Mishnah B'rurah*, Orach Chaim 253:70
110. *Mishnah B'rurah,* Orach Chaim 253:37
111. *Sha'ar HaTziyun* Orach Chaim 253:37
112. Cf. *Igrot Moshe*, Orach Chaim Volume IV 74 — Bishul. See chapter five concerning this point.

SECTION II

Automatically Heating Food on Shabbat

Introduction		59
Chapter 1	Automatic Cooking and Gerama	61
Chapter 2	A "Preparatory Cooking Act"	65
Chapter 3	Using an Electric Time Clock for Shabbat	69
Chapter 4	Automatic Cooking and *mechaze Ki-mevashel*	75
Chapter 5	Automatic Cooking and "Stoking the Coals"	77
Chapter 6	Reheating Fully Cooked Liquids	83
Chapter 7	A System for Automatically Heating Food on Shabbat	87

Introduction

The invention of the electric time clock enabled automatic cooking on electric heating devices. A time clock can activate the heating element of the device at some pre-determined time, thereby cooking (or reheating) any food previously placed upon it. The use of such a system on Shabbat raises several questions: Firstly, is the *Bishul* resulting from using this system directly attributable to the person placing food on the cold surface on Shabbat? To the person who sets the clock before Shabbat? Secondly, even if the *Bishul* cannot be directly attributed to either person, is it permitted to place food on Shabbat onto a cold surface that will subseqently be heated? Is it permitted to set a time clock to perform an action on Shabbat? Thirdly, if the food involved is fully cooked dry food, for which *Bishul* does not apply, do the Rabbinic cooking related prohibitions (discussed in Section I) apply to this type of system?

Chapter one introduces the concept of *Gerama*, indirect causation, specifically with respect to *Bishul*. Chapter two discusses the Halakhic status of an act that prepares the way for *Bishul*. Chapter three discusses the general use of a time clock on Shabbat. Chapter four indicates that using such a system on Shabbat does not "appear as cooking" for fully cooked dry food. Chapter five discusses the applicability of "stoking" to this system. Chapter six proves that reheating fully cooked liquids is equivalent to *Bishul* of uncooked food. Chapter seven describes a system that may be used to automatically reheat food on Shabbat.

Chapter 1
Automatic Cooking and *Gerama*

When food is placed on Shabbat upon a fire or a surface heated by fire, and left there for a given length of time, the Torah prohibition *Bishul* is transgressed.[1] The placement onto the surface and the subsequent cooking by the fire is considered one discrete occurrence directly attributable to the one who places the food. On the other hand, two separate occurrences are involved in automatic cooking. The first is the placement onto a cold surface, and the second is the automatic activation of the heater. The first occurrence alone does not cook, whereas the second occurrence is not attributable to the one who places the food.

The question therefore arises: Does placement onto a surface that will subsequently be heated automatically, transgress the prohibition of *Bishul* or any other prohibitions?

The *Chazon Ish*, a Halakhic authority of the first half of this century, considers such placement a *Gerama* of *Bishul*.[2] *Gerama*, indirect causation, is a highly complex issue that is primarily discussed apropos of the laws of damages. For the purposes of this section it may be postulated that whenever a *Ma'aseh*, a direct action, is required to fulfill or transgress a precept, doing a *Gerama* is insufficient. This principle is supported by the Talmud's comment on the fourth commandment, which expresses the prohibitions of Shabbat work: "'You shall do (*Ta'aseh*) no work[3]' — The Torah prohibits *Asiyah* (direct action), but not *Gerama*."[4]

If the Torah does not prohibit *Gerama*, then it does not prohibit placing food onto a surface that will subsequently be heated automatically. Despite the fact that certain types of *Gerama* on Shabbat are, nevertheless, Rabbinically prohibited (see Chapter 3), the

Chazon Ish does not consider this type of *Gerama* Rabbinically prohibited.

The determinant factor for whether or not a *Gerama* is Rabbinically prohibited, is the directness of the link between the consequences of an action and the initiator of that action. An example of a *Gerama* that is not Rabbinically prohibited can be brought from the laws of extinguishing a fire on Shabbat. Any fire that does not endanger human life may not be extinguished on Shabbat. Nevertheless, the Talmud permits placing new, water-filled clay jugs around the periphery of a fire, despite the fact that the spreading fire will burst the jugs, thereby enabling the water to extinguish the fire. The resultant extinction of the fire is so far removed from the action of placing the jugs that it is not Rabbinically prohibited.[5]

The *Chazon Ish* considers the placement of food onto a surface that will subsequently be heated automatically an even weaker *Gerama* than that of the clay jugs. Whereas the power of the fire is present when the jugs are placed, "the power of electricity is still absent" when the food is placed, and "the time clock does not yet have the power to start (the heat)." Nevertheless, concludes the *Chazon Ish*, since the *Rama*, the author of the glosses to the *Shulchan Arukh* that have become inseparable from the *Shulchan Arukh*, in accordance with the ruling of the *Mordechai* of the late Rishonim era, permits placing the jugs only to prevent damage,[6] the *Gerama* of placing food is also permitted only to "prevent damage."[7]

Rabbi Frank, a contemporary of the *Chazon Ish*, contests this approach based upon his interpretation of the laws of *Gerama*. He compares placing the food to placing the private property of another near a fire that subsequently spreads and damages that property. Just as the placer of the property is responsible for the damage subsequently caused by the fire, he feels that the placer of the food should also be responsible for the *Bishul* subsequently caused by the heat.[8]

A differentation between the two cases can be made, however. Whereas the fire exists when the property is placed near it, no heat exists when the food is placed. *Tosfot* makes a similar differentiation, ruling that a person is not responsible for placing the property of another near a potentially damaging power, if the means used by the power to damage does not yet exist. The example given by Tosfot is placing a bound animal near a venomous snake. Since the snake (the potentially damaging power) produces the means to damage (the venom) while biting the animal, at the time of placement the means used by the snake to damage does not yet exist. Consequently, the placer is not responsible for the damage to the bound animal.[9] Similarly, the means for cooking the food does not exist at the time of placement, and, consequently, the placement should be permitted.

Rabbi Frank, however, considers placing the food worse than placing a bound animal near a snake. In his view, electric potential in the circuit does exist at the time of placement, unlike the snake venom that requires a new action (a snake bite) to bring it into existance. As a result, he considers placing food onto a surface that will subsequently be heated automatically a transgression of the prohibition of *Bishul*.[8]

This view is difficult to comprehend. If venom, stored in the body of a snake, is considered by *Tosfot* "Not yet in this world," then certainly electric heat is "not yet in this world." The current that results from the rapid movement of the electrons must still be produced as well. Even the electric potential present at the moment of placement is not the same as the electric potential present at the moment of activation by the time clock. Furthermore, as demonstrated in *Ma'aseh U'Gerama Ba'Halakha,* the publication of the Institute for Science and Halakha on *Gerama*, it is only prohibited on Shabbat to bring the acting power in proximity of the object upon which it must act. Bringing the object such as food, in proximity of the power, such as the surface that will be automatically heated, could be permitted.[10]

The *Minchat Yitzchak* of Jerusalem, also contests the conclusion of the *Chazon Ish*. In his view, whenever food is placed upon a hot surface on Shabbat a *Gerama*-like action is involved since the power cooking is the fire and the placement itself does not cook. Since placement on a hot surface nevertheless transgresses the prohibition of *Bishul*, *Gerama* of *Bishul* is manifestly prohibited. Accordingly, *Gerama*, as in automatic cooking, should also be prohibited.[11]

Yet the *Minhat Yitzhak* himself indicates that placing onto a hot surface was the method of cooking used during the erection of the Tabernacle. Since the actions used for erection of the Tabernacle are those actions considered "Shabbat work," (see General Introduction) the *Gerama* nature of that action is irrelevant. On the other hand, once "Shabbat work" is defined by the actions performed to erect the Tabernacle, then *Gerama* of those defined actions is like any other *Gerama*. Accordingly, placing food where it will be subsequently cooked automatically could be permitted. Furthermore, as indicated in the beginning of the chapter, normal *Bishul* is one continuous action directly attributable to the placer of the food. Since placing food onto a cold surface is an action separate from the automatic activation of the heater, the *Bishul* is not directly attributable to the placer of the food, and can perhaps, be permitted.

In summation: The view of the *Chazon Ish*, that placing food onto a surface that will subsequently be heated automatically is a *Gerama* of *Bishul*, has been upheld. Nevertheless, this *Gerama* is only permitted to prevent damage. Whether or not other prohibitions are involved in such placement, however, has not been discussed.

Chapter 2
A "Preparatory Cooking Act"

Whether or not placing food onto a surface that will subsequently be heated automatically is a *Gerama* of *Bishul*, other serious Rabbinic prohibitions may be involved. The act of placement, without which *Bishul* could not have ocurred when the surface is heated, prepares the way for *Bishul*. If it can be shown that an act that prepares the way for *Bishul* is prohibited, then placing food onto a surface that will subsequently be heated automatically is prohibited as well.

The Talmud writes about a similar case: "if one brings the fire [on Shabbat] another brings wood, another places the pot, another brings water, another adds a spice, and another stirs, all are *chayav* [a legal term denoting culpability for punishment]... Did we not learn elsewhere the last is *chayav* and all the rest are *Patur* (the opposite of *chayav* — free of punishment)? There is no question: Here (the 'all are *chayav*' ruling) the fire was brought first, here (the 'all the rest are *Patur*' ruling) the fire was brought last."[12]

The *RaMBaM*, explains that "all who do an action necessary for the cooking process are said to cook."[13] Seemingly, however, the action must result directly in cooking. An action that does not directly result in cooking, unless a subsequent action occurs, is not *chayav*. But, is that action permitted?

Generally speaking, any Shabbat action ruled *Patur*, is *Patur, aval assur* — not *chayav*, but prohibited.[14] Accordingly, placing a pot onto an area to which fire will subsequently be brought, as well as the other enumerated actions, should be prohibited. Based on this point the *T'rumat HaDeshen,* a fifteenth century Rishon, prohibits placing food on Shabbat onto a cold winter heating stove that is to be lit by a gentile.[15] The *RaMA* concurs with this ruling[16] and the *Magen*

Avraham, a major seventeenth century commentary on the *Shulchan Arukh*, explains that such placement is "like one who places the pot and another who places the fire, where the first is *Patur* but prohibited."[17]

Unlike the Talmudic ruling, however, the actual cooking is done by a Gentile, for whom cooking on Shabbat is permitted. If the placement is prohibited nevertheless, then the prohibitory factor in common to both seems to be that the placement action prepares the way for subsequent cooking. Accordingly, whether or not the relationship between the placement and the subsequent cooking is one of *Gerama*, placing food in an area in which the food will subsequently be cooked is prohibited because it is a "preparatory cooking act."

The Beit Ephraim, in a turn of the century responsa, questions this approach. In his view, the *Patur* ruling of the Talmud need not mean *Patur* — but prohibited. Only the *Patur* rulings of a Mishnah are interpreted *Patur* — but prohibited, and this ruling does not originate in a Mishnah. Furthermore, even a Mishnaic *Patur* is ruled "but prohibited" only when some prohibitable action is performed. Placing a pot onto a surface where there is no fire and no reason to assume that a transgression will subsequently occur, is not a prohibitable action.

If this *Patur* ruling is to be interpreted "but prohibited," asserts the *Beit Ephraim*, then the circumstances of placement must be different than hitherto understood. It would have to be a group that had divided among themselves the various sub-acts that comprise cooking. Consequently, the one who places the food knows that as a result of his act fire will be brought, and that without his act *Bishul* could not occur. If he places the food, nevertheless, his act of placing abets a sinner (the one who subsequently brings the fire) in his transgression. Since abetting a sinner in his transgression is prohibited, the placing is *Patur*, but prohibited.

On the other hand, a Gentile who lights a heating stove on Shabbat is not a "sinner", and placing food on that stove when cold, does not "abet a sinner in his transgression." Consequently, the *Beit Ephraim* feels that placing food on the winter stove should be permitted, even if the placer knows that a Gentile will subsequently light the stove. By extension, placing a food onto a surface to be subsequently heated automatically should also be permitted, since it does not "abet a sinner."

Nevertheless, the *Beit Ephraim* concludes that he is "unworthy of challenging a matter that came out of the mouth of such a great authority (the *Terumat HaDeshen*, specifically) when it was subsequently accepted by the the *RaMA* and other late authorities." Accordingly, he prohibits placement onto a heating stove that will subsequently be lit by a Gentile.[18]

The ruling for automatic cooking, however, could be more lenient. Any partnership in the cooking proces could be prohibited, regardless of whether the partner is a Jew or a Gentile, because it is common for one person to bring food and another fire. Consequently, the placement appears to be a part of the cooking process. On the other hand, the normal cooking process never includes placing food onto a cold surface in which an electric time clock activates a heater to cook the food. Consequently, perhaps such placing could be permitted. Nevertheless, in the absence of proof that the *Terumat haDeshen*, *RaMA*, and *Magen Avraham* concur with this differentiation, the placement must be prohibited.

To summarize: The Talmud rules that when one person places a pot and a second places the fire the first is *Patur*. The *Terumat HaDeshen, RaMA*, and others interpret this: "*Patur* but prohibited" because it is a "preparatory cooking act." Consequently, they prohibit placing food onto a stove that will subsequently be lit by a Gentile, and presumably they would prohibit placing food onto an area that will subsequently be heated automatically. Although the *Beit Ephraim* disagrees, and feels that only a placement that "abets a sinner" should be prohibited, he defers to the rulings of the *Terumat HaDeshen* and *RaMA*. Accordingly, it seems prohibited to place on Shabbat onto an area that will subsequently be heated automatically.

Chapter 3
Using an Electric Time Clock for Shabbat

The previous chapters have examined the permissibility of placing food on Shabbat onto a surface that will subsequently be heated automatically. A more basic question, however, is whether or not an electric time clock may be used to do work on Shabbat. In general terms, the question may be posed as follows: May circumstances be arranged before Shabbat in a manner in which work will be initiated automatically on Shabbat?

To answer this question, two Talmudic rulings of the Mishnaic period must be analyzed. The first ruling is the prohibition of placing wheat in a water mill before Shabbat if the milling is to continue on Shabbat.[19] The second ruling is the prohibition of arranging a system before Shabbat in which oil drips from an eggshell to add fuel to a lamp on Shabbat.[20] These rulings are explained differently by the Jerusalem Talmud and by the Babylonian Talmud. The permissibility of an electric time clock is dependent upon which explanation is accepted.

The Jerusalem Talmud bases the two prohibitions on one principle: It is prohibited to initiate before Shabbat an action relating to a substance composed of discrete parts. The reason for this prohibition is that each discrete part involves a distinct action, and some of these distinct actions will occur exclusively on Shabbat. Accordingly, since some of the grains will be milled exclusively on Shabbat and some of the drops of oil will be burned exclusively on Shabbat, these two cases are prohibited.[21] Similarly, it should be prohibited to arrange circumstances so that an action be initiated on Shabbat.

On the other hand, although the Babylonian Talmud ascribes such a prohibition to Beit Shamai,[22] no such prohibition is mentioned in conjunction with the Halakhically binding view of Beit Hillel. It explains that the dripping oil is prohibited to prevent the likelihood of using the oil for other purposes, which can involve extinction of the fire.[23] There is a controversy concerning the reason for the other prohibition. One view bases the prohibition on the noise of the mill, which leads people to assume that work is being done on Shabbat. The other view bases the prohibition on a requirement that Jewish property "rest" on Shabbat (*Shevitat Kelim*).[24]

With the exception of one minority view[25] rejected by the later authorities, no major Halakhic authority requires Jewish property to rest on Shabbat.[26] The other two Halakhic problems, using the oil and the noise of the mill, do not apply to automatically initiating work on Shabbat (for work that is not noisy). Accordingly, since in a conflict between the Jerusalem Talmud and Babylonian Talmud the view of the latter is accepted, automatically initiating work on Shabbat should be permitted.

However, Rabbi Auerbach of Jerusalem attempts to demonstrate that the Babylonian Talmud can agree with the view of the Jerusalem Talmud in certain circumstances. He cites the ruling of the Mishnah that "a vessel may be placed underneath a lamp to catch sparks. But one may not put water into that [vessel] for that would be *kibuy* [extinguishing]."[27] The Babylonian Talmud extends this prohibition to placing the vessel before Shabbat, as well, "for that hastens the extinction."[28] *Rashi* and *Tosfot* explain that "hastening the extinction" refers to the increased likelihood of adding water on Shabbat were it permitted to add water before Shabbat.[29] On the other hand, both the *RIF*, in his tenth century codification, and the *RaMBaM*, who would normally clarify such important modifications, cite the ruling verbatim in their codifications.[30] This implies that they accept the prohibition of "hastening the extinction" literally. If so, then they prohibit placing water before Shabbat, because that causes work (extinction) to be initiated on Shabbat. Rabbi Auerbach claims that the basis for this prohibition is the previously cited view of the Jerusalem Talmud.

If the Babylonian Talmud agrees with the view of the Jerusalem Talmud, however, then why was it necessary to find alternate explanations for the prohibitions of the mill and the oil? Rabbi Auerbach explains that the Babylonian Talmud disagrees with the application of the principle to these prohibitions but not with the principle. According to him, the Babylonian Talmud views all the drops of oil and all the grains of wheat as one unit, unlike the Jerusalem Talmud, which considers each drop and each grain a discrete unit. Accordingly, each drop of oil and each grain of wheat is part of a unit upon which work was initiated before Shabbat. Since the work on the unit was initiated before Shabbat, the view of the Jerusalem Talmud does not apply. On the other hand, each random spark that falls from an oil lamp is independent of any other spark. Accordingly, placing water underneath the lamp before Shabbat is prohibited because the act of extinguishing a spark is initiated on Shabbat. Similarly, it should be prohibited to set a time clock before Shabbat to automatically initiate an action on Shabbat.[31]

There are two problems with this interpretation. The first problem is that the same Rav Yossi of the Jerusalem Talmud who explains the ruling for the mill and for the oil-filled eggshell, gives a different explanation for the ruling for the sparks. In his view, the prohibition of placing water applies *only* to Shabbat itself, and the reason for the prohibition is that placing the water in the vessel indirectly causes the extinction (*Geram Kibuy*) of the sparks.[32] This implies that even Rabbi Yossi is not concerned with the fact that placing water before Shabbat results in the initiation of extinction on Shabbat.

The second problem is that another Mishnah, binding on both the Babylonian Talmud and on the Jerusalem Talmud, permits setting up an animal trap before Shabbat despite the fact that trapping (*Tzad*), a Torah prohibition, results on Shabbat.[33] Here, too, it is permitted to arrange before Shabbat an action to be initiated on Shabbat. If so, then why does the Jerusalem Talmud permit setting up a trap and placing water underneath an oil lamp, before Shabbat, and yet prohibit starting a mill and dripping oil from an eggshell into a lamp before Shabbat?

A possible differentiation between the actions permitted before Shabbat and those prohibited, reverses the logic of Rabbi Auerbach. Accordingly, initiating work on a unit composed of parts before Shabbat is prohibited if work on parts of that unit will continue on Shabbat, whereas work initiated on a unit on Shabbat itself if permitted. This is because the work continuing on Shabbat is observably connected to the iniator of the work, whereas work that is automatically initiated on Shabbat is not. This observable connection is Rabbinically prohibited because it appears to be Shabbat work. Thus, the milling of a discrete grain of wheat on Shabbat, as well as the dripping of a discrete drop of oil on Shabbat, is prohibited because of the observable connection to the personal action that was initiated before Shabbat. On the other hand, the animal is trapped automatically on Shabbat, and the spark is extinguished automatically on Shabbat. These actions are permitted because they are seen as separate from the action of setting the trap before Shabbat, or placing the water before Shabbat.

According to this differentiation, even the Jerusalem Talmud permits setting a time clock before Shabbat to initiate work on Shabbat. Even without this differentiation, it is quite difficult to maintain that the unstated intention of the Babylonian Talmud is based upon a ruling from the Jerusalem Talmud, that itself is qualified by permission in two cases. Certainly, the explicit clarification of *Rashi* and *Tosfot* cannot be reconciled with Rabbi Auerbach's approach, whereas the problematic approach of the *RIF* and the *RaMBaM*, are insufficient basis for such an approach. Furthermore, the major commentaries on the *Shulchan Arukh* base the prohibition on the view of *Rashi* and *Tosfot*,[34] and no major commentary supports the view of Rabbi Auerbach. Consequently, an electric time clock may be set before Shabbat to initiate an action on Shabbat, provided that no other prohibitions are involved.

Rabbi Feinstein of New York, however, prohibits using an electric time clock for Shabbat work. In his view, it "cheapens" the Shabbat and contradicts the spirit of respect for Shabbat (*Kavod HaShabbat*). He nevertheless, permits its use for turning lights on and off on Shabbat for two reasons. The first reason is based upon the fact that many authorities permit telling a Gentile to turn the lights on and off on Shabbat under certain circumstances. Setting a clock before Shabbat should be similar to telling a Gentile to do work on Shabbat. The second reason is that the lights are turned on for the respect of Shabbat.[35]

If that is so, then perhaps a time clock could also be used to reheat (as opposed to "cook") food on Shabbat. Many authorities also permit telling a Gentile to reheat food on Shabbat.[36] If that is sufficient reason to permit using a time clock for lights, it should also be sufficient reason to permit using a time clock for reheating. Furthermore, eating hot food on Shabbat is one of the definitions of "Respect of Shabbat."[37] Thus, despite the fact that Rabbi Feinstein's prohibition of a time clock was specifically for turning on an oven, his reasons for permitting a time clock for light seem to apply to reheating food as well.

In summation: The Babylonian Talmud and the Jerusalem Talmud give conflicting reasons for prohibiting certain actions that occur automatically on Shabbat. Whereas the reason given by the Jerusalem Talmud seems to prohibit the use of an automatic time clock, the reasons given by the Babylonian Talmud, upon which the Halakhah is based, do not. Rabbi Auerbach attempts to prove that the Babylonian Talmud can, for circumstances that apply to a time clock, agree with the Jerusalem Talmud. Nevertheless, various rulings of the Jerusalem Talmud itself contest this conclusion, and no major commentary directly supports it. Rabbi Feinstein considers the use of a time clock a "cheapening" of Shabbat. Nevertheless, the same reasons that he uses to permit using a time clock for lights, apply to using a time-clock for reheating food on Shabbat. Thus, setting a time-clock before Shabbat to reheat food on Shabbat seems permitted.

Chapter 4
Automatic Cooking and *mechaze Ki-mevashel*

The end of the last chapter presented a subtle shift of emphasis. Until that point "cooking," the Torah prohibition *Bishul*, was discussed. Because of the objection of Rabbi Feinstein, however, reheating food, rather than cooking food, was discussed. As indicated in Section I, reheating fully cooked solid food does not transgress the Torah prohibition of *Bishul*, but can transgress various Rabbinic prohibitions. If no Torah prohibitions are transgressed, then the problems discussed in the first two chapters do not apply. Placing fully cooked cold food onto a surface that will subsequently be heated automatically may be a *Gerama* of the subsequent reheating. That, however, is a *Gerama* of a Rabbinic prohibition, which is permitted by many authorities.[38] It cannot be considered a "preparatory cooking act" either, since "cooking" — *Bishul* — is never involved. Thus, the problems discussed in the first three chapters do not apply to automatically reheating cold solid foods.

Other problems, however, can apply to automatically reheating solid foods. Section I indicated that two categories of prohibitions can be involved when reheating cold solid food on Shabbat. One category is based upon "appearing as cooking," and the other upon "stoking the coals." This chapter deals with whether automatically reheating solid food "appears as cooking."

For placement to "appear as cooking" it must be equivalent in all respects to an action of *Bishul*. Due to technical differences in the food itself, *Bishul* is not transgressed when placing cold fully cooked food onto a hot surface, but it does "appear as *Bishul*." On the the other hand, placing food of any kind onto a cold surface is not an action of *Bishul*. If the surface is subsequently heated automatically, it is still not an action of *Bishul*, but, as indicated in Chapter 1, a *Gerama* of *Bishul*. Consequently, the placement does not "appear as cooking."

Even if placing food onto a surface that will subsequently be heated automatically is not considered a *Gerama*, the placement still does not "appear as cooking." If an action is not a *Gerama*, that merely means that there is direct personal responsibility for the results of the action. That, however, does not change the appearance of the action. Since at the time of placement the action did not "appear as cooking" because the surface was cold, it certainly cannot subseqently "appear as cooking" regardless of whether or not a *Gerama* is involved. Therefore, those prohibitions based upon "appearing as cooking" do not apply to placing cold fully cooked solid food on Shabbat onto a cold surface that will subsequently be heated automatically.

Chapter 5
Automatic Cooking and "Stoking the Coals"

It is still necessary to determine whether the prohibitions based upon "stoking the coals" apply to automatically heated food, (whether or not the food was fully cooked). This can be determined by examining the ruling for food placed on Shabbat onto an area for which "stoking" applies. If it can be shown that this ruling does not apply to food placed onto a cold surface that was subsequently heated, then it can be assumed that "stoking" does not apply to automatically heated food.

The ruling for food placed on Shabbat onto an area for which "stoking" applies (such as an "unswept" fire) is that it must be removed immediately.[39] Yet, if a gentile places food onto an "unswept" fire on Shabbat it need not be removed.[40] If it need not be removed from the fire then it can be assumed that the problem of "stoking" does not apply. The fact that the problem of "stoking" nevertheless applies when a Jew places food on such a fire, implies that the applicability of "stoking" is determined at the moment of placement. If a gentile places food on a fire, then since the problem of "stoking" does not apply to a gentile, the problem did not apply at the moment of placement and the food may remain on the fire. By extension, since a cold surface cannot be "stoked," "stoking" does not apply at the moment of placement onto a cold surface. Accordingly, "stoking" should not subsequently apply when there is heat, and the food should be permitted to remain.

An obvious differentiation can be made between the case of automatically cooked food and between the case of the food placed by the Gentile. Whereas in the former case, the food is placed by a Jew for whom the prohibitions of Shabbat apply, in the latter case the food is placed by a gentile for whom the prohibitions of Shabbat do not apply.

Consequently, even if there is no requirement to remove food placed by a Gentile, perhaps there is a requirement to remove food placed by a Jew onto a cold surface.

This differentiation is consistent with the ruling that uncooked food placed by a Jew onto an unswept *Kirah* before Shabbat (*Shehiyah*) must be removed on Shabbat.[41] Yet, both *Shehiyah* and *chazarah* are aimed at preventing the likelihood of "stoking" the coals, as discussed in Section I. The *Shehiyah* placement occurs before Shabbat when placement is permitted, and the food must nevertheless be removed if there is a likelihood of subsequent "stoking." Why, then, is it unnecessary to remove the food of a permitted *chazarah* placement (such as placement on Shabbat by a gentile) when there is the same likelihood of subsequent "stoking?"

To answer this it is necessary to differentiate between the prohibitions of *Shehiyah* and *chazarah*. It was explained in Section I that the heightened involvement in the cooking process represented by the act of re-placement on Shabbat renders the likelihood of "stoking" greater for *chazarah* than for *Shehiyah*. As a result, *Shehiyah* can be permitted once the food is cooked to *ma'akhal Ben Derusai*, whereas *chazarah* can be prohibited even for fully cooked food. If, however, the placement act does not represent heightened involvement in the cooking process, then *chazarah* should be no more stringent than *Shehiyah*. Consequently, if food cooked at least to *ma'akhal Ben Derusai* is placed onto a cold surface, or if it is placed by a gentile onto any surface there is seemingly no heightened involvement in the cooking process that could lead to "stoking." In such cases, therefore, the food should not have to be removed.

The *Magen Avraham*'s explanation of the *RaMA*'s permission of placing hot fully cooked food alongside the walls of a winter stove[42] is inconsistent with this interpretation. The *Magen Avraham* explains: "'Alongside the winter stove', but not on it, since it is not swept nor [its coals] covered with ash. The text of the *RaMA* indicates that placement on it is prohibited even before lighting [the stove]. We prohibit it to prevent the likelihood of stoking the coals since in the end there will be fire inside..."[43]

Since, according to the *Magen Avraham* it is prohibited for a Jew even to place fully cooked food onto a cold area that will subsequently be lit by a Gentile, placing food on a cold area that will subsequently be heated automatically should also be prohibited.

This view of the *Magen Avraham* is somewhat problematic. Why is the problem of stoking the coals not applied to food placed by a gentile onto a stove that he will subsequently light? Is there a greater likelihood of "stoking" food placed by a Jew onto a cold stove than food placed by a gentile onto a cold stove?

This question can be answered with a cautious "yes." Perhaps the placement by a Jew indicates a heightened involvement in the food warming process. Since this heightened involvement could later result in stoking the coals, the placement is prohibited, and if placed, the food must be removed. On the other hand, the placement by a gentile indicates no heightened involvement of a Jew in the food warming process. Consequently, there is no reason to prevent the likelihood of "stoking" and the situation is comparable to *Shehiyah* of *ma'akhal Ben Derusai* food which need not be removed on Shabbat.

However, there could be one lenient factor for placing food onto a cold surface that will subsequently be heated automatically. The *Magen Avraham* concludes the above citation by explaining that it is nevertheless customary to place food on top of winter stoves on Shabbat before they are lit, because they have no opening on top.[44] The top, therefore, functions as a covering for the coals, thereby mitigating the likelihood of "stoking." Similarly, the "fire" of an electric heater is generally covered. It could then have the same ruling as placing onto a cold winter stove. On the other hand, "stoking the coals" is generally viewed as the equivalent of adjusting the heat level on a modern heater (see Section 1). If that is the case, then the lenient ruling for the winter stove would not apply to automatic heating, unless the problem of "stoking" is solved as discussed in Section I.

II

Before concluding this chapter, one important dissenting view must be discussed: that of the *Chazon Ish*. According to the *Chazon Ish*, it is necessary to remove all food placed on a fire on Shabbat to prevent the likelihood of "stoking", whether the food was placed by a Jew, a

Gentile, or even a monkey. Consequently, he questions the ruling of the *RaMA* that permits telling a gentile on Shabbat to place the food onto a winter stove that the gentile with subsequently light to heat the house. In his view, it should nevertheless be necessary to remove the food once the fire is lit to prevent the likelihood of stoking the coals.

To answer this question the *Chazon Ish* explains that any placement of food onto a fire on Shabbat is considered *chazarah* regardless of who places the food. If the fire is not "swept or covered with ash" (see Section I) the food must then be removed to prevent the likelihood of "stoking." On the other hand, placing food onto a *cold* surface does not involve a prohibited *chazarah*, since "stoking" a cold surface is impossible. When the stove is subsequently lit, and "stoking" is possible, the food is already there. Since the Gentile was permitted to place the food, when the Jew allows it to remain on the fire it is *Shehiyah*. Consequently, if the food is cooked to the point for which *Shehiyah* is permitted (see Section I) it need not be removed from the fire.

On the other hand, concludes the *Chazon Ish*:
"If the fire must subsequently come to the oven, as with an electric machine set before Shabbat [for the heat] to come at a specific time, it would be prohibited to place into that oven before the fire comes even fully cooked food that is warm, as is the prohibition of *chazarah*, since it is considered a Shabbat placement. And even if placing onto an oven that will be lit by a gentile is not considered a Shabbat placement [but *Shehiyah*] that is because an action of free choice is still missing [the gentile can choose to light or not to light the oven]. But here, where the heat will automatically come, it would seem to be considered a [prohibited] Shabbat placement."[45]

This conclusion of the *Chazon Ish* is difficult to understand. When the Gentile lights the stove he is merely performing the job for which he was hired. "Freedom of choice" should be irrelevant to defining a placement onto a cold surface as *Shehiyah* or *chazarah*. The fact that after the placement there is freedom of choice affects the degree of direct culpability (*Gerama* terminology, see Chapter one) that the placer has for the subsequent cooking. Accordingly, when an action must automatically follow, the culpability of the initiator is greater than when an action will follow depending upon the free will of another. On the other hand, the likelihood of "stoking" is unaffected. If the time of placement is the qualifying factor for prohibition, then in either case the oven is cold at the time of placement, "stoking" is inapplicable, and the food could remain. Conversely, if the time of heat commencement is the qualifying factor for prohibition, then in either case "stoking " could apply, and the food should be removed. It is, therefore, difficult to understand why the *Chazon Ish* could consider placing food onto an area to be lit by a gentile a function of *Shehiyah*, and placing food onto an area to be heated automatically a function of *chazarah*.

Whether or not the view of the *Chazon Ish* is accepted, placing food on Shabbat onto a cold area that will subsequently be heated automatically is prohibited. According to the *Chazon Ish* the prohibition is that of *chazarah* despite the fact that the placement is onto a cold surface. According to the *Magen Avraham* the prohibition is based upon the heightened involvement of the placer in the heating process which could lead to "stoking," which in the case of an electric food warmer is adjusting the heat level.

Chapter 6
Reheating Fully Cooked Liquids

Before applying the conclusions of the previous chapters to designing a system that could be used to automatically reheat food on Shabbat, one ruling must be clarified: The prohibition of reheating liquids on Shabbat. Is that prohibition a Torah prohibition or a Rabbinic prohibition? If it is a Torah prohibition, then automatically reheating liquids involves the problems discussed in the first two chapters. On the other hand, if it is a Rabbinic prohibition then, as indicated in chapter 4, those problems do not apply (even if the problem of the previous chapter does).

The prohibition of reheating liquids is expressed "*Yesh Bishul Achar Bishul BeLach*"[46] ("There is *Bishul* after a liquid is cooked"). The term *Bishul* is generally reserved for the Torah precept, implying that the Torah precept is transgressed even when fully cooked liquids are reheated. Similarly, the language of the *Shulchan Arukh*, "A Fully cooked [liquid] food can have in it [when reheated the prohibition of] *Bishul* when it cools off,"[47] implies that it "has in it" the Torah prohibition when reheated.

On the other hand, the *RaMA* later comments: "And the more lenient say that whenever it [fully cooked liquid] is not placed upon the fire or the *Kirah* itself, but only alongside it [avoiding the likelihood of "stoking"], then it is permitted even if it cooled. And the custom is to rule leniently provided that it did not fully cool off."[48]

Many authorities cite this ruling as proof that the *RaMA* considers reheating fully cooked liquids a Rabbinic prohibition.[49] It seems inappropriate to "rule leniently provided that it did not fully cool off" unless reheating liquids is a Rabbinic prohibition. Were it a Torah prohibition the ruling would presumably be more stringent, since doubtful Torah rulings are ruled stringently (*Safek De'orayta LeChumra*).⁵⁰

Nevertheless, another ruling of the *RaMA* indicates even more clearly that the prohibition of reheating liquids is a Torah prohibition. Chapter two mentioned the ruling of the *RaMA* that prohibits placing cold fully cooked liquid onto a winter stove on Shabbat that will be lit by a gentile.⁵¹ As indicated there, the source for this ruling is the *Terumat HaDeshen*'s prohibition of a "preparatory cooking act" which applies when Torah *Bishul* will follow. If the *RaMA* considers placement of cold fully cooked liquid a "preparatory cooking act," then the subsequent heating of the liquid must be a "cooking" — *Bishul* — act. Thus, reheating cold liquids must be a Torah prohibition.

How can this be reconciled with the previously cited *RaMA* that "rules leniently if it did not fully cool off?" An analysis of the difference between cooking liquids and cooking solids offers a possible reconciliation.

Cooking solids transgresses the Torah prohibition of *Bishul* when cooked to the point of *ma'akhal Ben Derusai*.⁵² (See Section I). Food is inedible before that point whether or not it is hot, and somewhat edible after that point whether or not it is hot. Accordingly, reheating food (specifically fully cooked food) does not affect the determining factor for *Bishul*. On the other hand, cooking liquids transgresses the Torah prohibition of *Bishul* when cooked to the temperature of *Yad Soledet Bo*⁵³ (See Section IV). At that point the properties of a liquid (for example: water) change to make the liquid usable where cold liquid is not usable. When the temperature reverts to what it was, the liquid is no longer usable. Perhaps, however, the changed properties of the liquid do not fully revert to what they were until the liquid fully cools. Consequently, reheating liquid that retains some warmth need not transgress the Torah prohibitions of *Bishul*.

In summation: the phrase *Yesh Bishul Achar Bishul BeLach*, as well as the ruling of the *Shulchan Arukh*, implies that the Torah prohibition *Bishul* is transgressed when liquids are reheated. Many authorities feel that the *RaMA*, who rules leniently for reheating liquids that did not fully cool off, considers the prohibition a Rabbinic prohibition. Nevertheless, the *RaMA*'s prohbition of placing cold fully cooked liquids onto a cold winter stove, based upon the ruling of the *Terumat HaDeshen* challenges that interpretation. Since the previously cited lenient ruling can be explained in an alternate manner, it would seem that reheating cold fully cooked liquids on Shabbat transgresses the Torah prohibition of *Bishul*.

Chapter 7
A System for Automatically Heating Food on Shabbat

This section discussed the halakhic problems that can be associated with automatically heating food on Shabbat. The problems may be summarized as follows:
1. Placing food onto a surface in which *Bishul* will later take place is a *Gerama* of the *Bishul* that is normally prohibited.
2. Placing food onto a surface in which *Bishul* will later take place is prohibited as a "preparatory cooking act."
3. Using an electric time clock to perform Shabbat work can, according to some authorities, "cheapen" the spirit of Shabbat.
4. a) According to the *Magen Avraham*, the heightened involvement of a Jew in the food warming process could lead to a Jew "stoking the coals" — adjusting the temperature.

b) According to the *Chazon Ish* any Shabbat placement on a surface that will be hot is prohibited to a Jew.

It was shown that the first three problems do not apply to food for which *Bishul* does not apply. Consequently, they do not apply to fully cooked non-liquid food. It is nevertheless prohibited to place that food where it will be automatically heated because of problem number four.

Problem 4a is easily solved by designing the heater so that temperature adjustment is impossible. As discussed in Section I, that is the equivalent of "sealing an oven with clay" which precludes the likelihood of stoking the coals. The *Chazon Ish* might nevertheless prohibit such automatic heating, both because he applies "sealed with clay" only to *Shehiyah* and not to *chazarah*, (see Section I) and because he prohibits any Shabbat placement that results in heating.

A pre-Shabbat placement, however, should be permitted by the

Chazon Ish. But how is the food to be kept from spoiling from the time of a pre-Shabbat placement until the time of Shabbat lunch? By refrigeration! There are commercially available refrigerator-heaters that both refrigerate and heat food. A time-clock could be set before Shabbat to automatically stop the refrigerator, and to heat the food before the Shabbat meal.

Additional modifications are necessary. No circuits should close or open, nor should any electric change occur as a result of opening or closing the door. Accordingly, care should be taken that the lights or bells that indicate the completion of the heating cycle should not be affected by opening the door. In addition, an electromagnetic lock should lock the door whenever the heater operates to avoid affecting the thermostat (see Section V) as well as to prevent non-observant kitchen help from adding food while the heater operates.

Various modifications of this principle are possible. One of these modifications can even be adapted to home use. Fully cooked frozen dry food may be placed before Shabbat into an electric oven and surrounded with ice packs. The food would maintain an acceptable temperature until a pre-set time clock activates the heater to reheat the food. The individual, unlike a non-observant kitchen worker, would not put food into the oven while the heat was on, and would not need an electromagnetic lock. In fact, to avoid problems related to the thermostat (see Section V) the oven should preferably not be opened until the heating cycle is complete.

Regardless of the modification used, this principle allows eating fresh, hot food on Shabbat. Not only is this important on the commercial level where hygienic and culinary concerns requires fresh hot food (as opposed to food left over a covered fire), but it is important on the individual level as well. It is considered a mitzvah to eat hot food on Shabbat,[54] and any method that aids in fulfilling this mitzvah in halakhically acceptable ways is beneficial.

This method is Halakhically acceptable because it solves all four problems mentioned above. The problem of gravy — a liquid — that usually accompanies cooked food and for which *Bishul* does apply is of little concern, provided that there is a majority of non-liquid. Not only do some authorities permit reheating food under those circumstances,[55] but in this case no personal reheating action is done on Shabbat. Any personal actions are performed before the onset of Shabbat. Thus, food could be automatically heated with this system on Shabbat in commercial institutions as well as at home.

Section II

1. *Rambam* Shabbat Laws 9:1, 2, 5; *Shulchan Arukh* Orach Chaim 318:3
2. *Chazon Ish* Orach Chaim 38:3
3. Ex. 20:10
4. TB Shabbat 120b
5. TB Shabbat 120a
6. *Mordekhai,* Shabbat 22; *Rama,* Orach Chaim 334:22
7. *Chazon Ish* Orach Chaim 38:3
8. *Shut HarTzvi,* Orach Chaim I:136
9. *Tosfot* Bava Kama 56a s.v. *I'leima*; *Tosfot* Sanhedrin 77a s.v. *Sof*
10. *Ma'aseh U'Gerama Ba'Halakhah* II, 84:9. Cf. *Igrot Mosheh* Orach Chaim IV, 60
11. *Shut Minchat Yizchak,* Vol. 4,26
12. TB Beizah 34a
13. *Rambam* Shabbat Laws 9:4
14. TB Shabbat 3a
15. *T'rumat HaDeshen* 64
16. *Rama* Orach Chaim 253:5
17. *Magen Avraham* Orach Chaim 253:41
18. *Shut Beit Ephraim* Orach Chaim 21
19. TB Shabbat 18a; TJ Shabbat 1:5
20. Mishnayot Shabbat 2:4
21. TJ Shabbat 1:5; TJ Shabbat 2:4; also see commentaries of *Korban Edah* and *P'nei Mosheh*
22. TB Shabbat 18a
23. TB Shabbat 29b. See *Rashi* s.v. *She'tehei*, and *Rosh* Beiza 2:17
24. TB Shabbat 18a
25. *Rokay'ach* cited in *Beit Yosef* Orach Chaim 246 s.v. *Tanu*
26. *Tur* Orach Chaim 252; *Shulchan Arukh* Orach Chaim 252:1 and commentary of *Gera*. See also *Bach* on Tur Orach Chaim 246
27. Mishnayot Shabbat 3:6
28. TB Shabbat 47b
29. *Rashi* Shabbat 47b s.v. *Ela; Tosfot* Shabbat 47b s.v. *Mipnei*
30. *Rif* end of chapter 3 of Shabbat; *Rambam,* Shabbat Laws 5:13

31. *Me'orei Eish* chapter 4
32. TJ Shabbat 3:8, see commentary of *P'nei Mosheh*
33. Mishnayot Shabbat 1:6
34. *Taz,* Orach Chaim 265:2; *Magen Avraham,* Orach Chaim 265:7
35. *Igrot Moshe,* Orach Chaim IV 60
36. *Pri Megadim, Eshel Avraham,* Orach Chaim 253:38; *Sha'arei T'shuvah,* Orach Chaim 318:6; *Biur Halakhah* Orach Chaim 353:5 s.v. *Le'Hachem.*
37. *Rama,* Orach Chaim 257:8
38. *Yeshu'ot Ya'akov,* Orach Chaim 334:7; *Yavin Da'at* Kuntres G'ram Hama'alot 217; *HaChashmal Le'or HaHalakhah* 3:5; *Shut Chelkat Ya'akov* I:50; etc. Actually, no Rabbinic cooking prohibition is involved, even if *Shehiyah* and *Chazarah* are involved.
39. *Shulchan Arukh* Orach Chaim 253:1; *Magen Avraham* Orach Chaim 253:2
40. *Rama,* Orach Chaim 253:5
41. *Shulchan Arukh Orach Chaim* 253:1
42. *Rama,* Orach Chaim 253:4
43. *Magen Avraham,* Orach Chaim 253:43
44. *ibid.*
45. *Chazon Ish* Orach Chaim 37:21
46. *Tur,* Orach Chaim 318
47. *Shulchan Arukh,* Orach Chaim 318:4
48. *Rama,* Orach Chaim 318:15
49. *Minhat Kohen,* Mishmeret HaShabbat 2; *Eglei Tal,* Milekhet O'feh 55:5; *Chazon Ish,* Orach Chaim Hilkhot Shabbat 37:13, etc.
50. *TB Beizah* 3b
51. *Rama* Orach Chaim 253:5
52. *Rambam* Shabbat Laws 9:5
53. *Shulchan Arukh,* Orach Chaim 318:14
54. *HaMa'or,* Shabbat 3, end of s.v. *V'Im Tish'al; Rama,* Orach Chaim 257:8
55. *Magen Avraham,* 318:40; *Pri Megadim,* Eshel Avraham 318:40

SECTION III

An Alternate System for Re-heating Food on Shabbat

Introduction		95
Chapter 1	*Kli Sheni*	97
Chapter 2	Placing Pots of Food into a *Kli Sheni*	103
Chapter 3	A Warming Bath for Reheating Food on Shabbat	105

Introduction

Serving hot food on Shabbat in hotels and other large institutions raises serious Halakhic problems. These problems include *Bishul, Havarah, Shehiyah, chazarah* and *mechaze Ki-mevashel.* (See Section I) Avoiding these problems by leaving the food on warmers (on a covered fire) for the entire Shabbat is generally unacceptable for hygienic and culinary reasons. One possible solution, the refrigerator-heater, was discussed in the previous section. This section discusses a different solution based upon the principle of *Kli Sheni*, the vessel into which hot water is poured. This solution is more compatible with the food warming systems used in many institutions.

Chapter one discusses the Halakhic status of adding cold water into a *Kli Sheni* on Shabbat. Chapter two discusses warming pots of food in a *Kli Sheni* bath on Shabbat. Chapter 3 indicates various practical problems that result when using a *Kli Sheni* warming bath, and describes a system that solves these problems. The systems described are fully acceptable systems for preparing hot food on Shabbat.

Chapter 1
Kli Sheni

A vessel containing the hot water that was boiled in it, is called a *Kli Rishon* — first vessel — whether it is on the fire or off the fire. Cooking food in the hot water of a *Kli Rishon* that is off the fire is equivalent to cooking food that is on the fire, and transgresses the Torah prohibition of *Bishul*.[1] When the water in a *Kli Rishon* is transferred to a second vessel, the second vessel is called a *Kli Sheni*. Since the transfer to a *Kli Sheni* reduces the temperature of the water, the ruling for a *Kli Sheni* is less stringent than for a *Kli Rishon*.

The ruling for a *Kli Sheni* is, however, quite complex. It is based on a difficult Talmudic passage explained by the commentaries in conflicting ways. An analysis of the passage and the conflicting views of the commentaries will clarify the ruling for a *Kli Sheni*.

The Talmud rules: "In a bath... cold water may not be [poured] into hot water."[2] *Rashi* and the *RaN* explain that the bath is a *Kli Rishon*, and thus, the prohibition of pouring cold water into the bath is the Torah prohibition of *Bishul*. On the other hand, they permit pouring cold water into a *Kli Sheni*.[3]

Tosfot rejects this approach. In his view, the fact that the Talmud does not say "In a *Kli Rishon*... cold water may not be poured into hot water," indicates that the prohibitory factor is that it is a bath. A bath is "very hot, and it is necessary to guard against the viewer assuming that it is a *Kli Rishon*." Accordingly, the sages forbade adding cold water to a hot bath even thought the bath is a *Kli Sheni*.[4] Presumably, this prohibition applies to any hot *Kli Sheni* that can be mistaken for a *Kli Rishon*.

A further complication of this issue results from the *RaMBaM*'s unclear formulation of this ruling. He states: "The bath of a bathhouse that is filled with hot water cannot have cold water added to it, since it was greatly heated. He may similarly not put a flask of oil in [the bath], since it is as if he cooks it."[5]

On the one hand, the *RaMBaM,* seems to consider the bath a *Kli Sheni* to which cold water may not be added "since it was greatly heated." On the other hand, he seems to consider the bath a *Kli Rishon* into which one may "not put a flask of oil since it is as if he cooks it."

The classic commentaries on the *RaMBaM,* differ in their explanation of his intention. The *Magid Mishnah*, a commentary of the late Rishonim period, gives a seemingly incomplete explanation. He writes:

"... And this bath is a *Kli*... The reason that it is forbidden to put cold water into its hot [water], is because its water is for bathing and it is greatly heated. That is why the *RaMBaM,* states 'the bath of a bathhouse'.[6]"

Both the *BaCh,* in his seventeenth century commentary to the *Tur*,[7] and his son-in-law, the *TaZ,* in his commentary to the *Shulchan Arukh*,[8] emend the text of the *Magid Mishnah* to read "... And this bath is a *Kli Sheni*..." In their view, the *Magid Mishnah* explains that the *RaMBaM*'s view is equivalent to the view of *Tosfot*: It is Rabbinically prohibited to pour cold water into a *Kli Sheni* bath "since it was greatly heated."

On the other hand, the other two classic commentaries on the *RaMBaM* explain that the *RaMBaM* considers the bath a *Kli Rishon*, although they differ in the application of this ruling. The *Kesef Mishnah* commentary, written by the author of the *Shulchan Arukh*, applies this ruling to any *Kli Rishon*. In his view, this ruling introduces the next ruling of the *RaMBaM* that "... cold water [may be poured] into hot water, providing that they are not in a *Kli Rishon* since it was greatly heated."[9]

Despite this ruling of the *RaMBaM* which explicitly refers to a *Kli Rishon* other than a bath, the *Lechem Mishnah*, a slightly later commentary on the *RaMBaM*, applies the bath ruling to a bath only. In his own view, the addition of the words "of a bathhouse" implies a differentiation between a *Kli Rishon* bath, into which cold water may not be added, and between other *Kli Rishon* into which cold water may be added.[10] Adding cold water to a *Kli Sheni* bath however, is permitted by him, as well as by the *Kesef Mishnah*.

The issue is further complicated by the fourteenth century codification, the *Tur*. He prohibits pouring cold water even into a *Kli Sheni* basin of hot water, because "since they are for bathing, presumably they are very hot, and the cold water mixed into them will be cooked."[11] This seems to contradict the conclusion reached by the Talmud that a "basin" differs from a "bath",[12] which implies that cold water may be added to a hot basin used for bathing.

The *Beit Yosef*, Rabbi Yosef Caro's commentary on the *Tur* which he later condensed into the *Shulchan Arukh*, presents two approaches to resolve this apparent contradiction. The first approach explains that the *Tur* considers the Talmudic "bath" a *Kli Sheni* into which cold water may not be added due to its characteristic of maintaining heat longer than other *Kli Sheni* such as a "basin." Nevertheless, due to our unfamiliarity with the salient characteristics that differentiate between the Talmudic "bath" and "basin," the *Tur* found it necessary to "prohibit (any) *Kli Sheni* used for bathing."[13]

If "unfamiliarity" is sufficient cause for prohibiting any *Kli Sheni* used for bathing, then putting cold water into a *Kli Sheni* bath must transgress a Torah prohibition. Otherwise, doubt based upon unfamiliarity would not prohibit a *Kli Sheni* basin, since doubt is generally insufficient cause for prohibiting an action that prevents possible transgression of a Rabbinic prohibition. It would, therefore, seem that the *Beit Yosef* understood the *Tur* as considering adding water to a *Kli Sheni* bath a Torah prohibition. This interpretation is further strengthened by the *Tur*'s words "will be cooked" — *Mitbashlin*.[14] This implies that the Torah prohibition of *Bishul* is transgressed when cold water is added to a *Kli Sheni* bath.

The second approach of the *Beit Yosef* understood the *Tur* as considering adding cold water into a *Kli Sheni* bath a transgression of a Rabbinic prohibition. The apparent contradiction of the ruling for "basin" is explained by this approach as follows: "Basin," as used by the Talmud, is the vessel which removes hot water from the Bath. Since the Bath is a *Kli Sheni*, the Basin is a further step removed, a *Kli Shelishi*. Accordingly, the talmudic differentiation between a "bath" and a "basin" is a differentiation between a *Kli Sheni* and a *Kli Shelishi*. Consequently, the *Tur* prohibits adding cold water into a *Kli Sheni* basin, as he prohibits adding water to any *Kli Sheni* used for bathing. On the other hand, the *Tur* could permit pouring cold water into a *Kli Shelishi* basin.[15]

The underlying premise in both approaches of the *Beit Yosef* is that there is a contradiction between the conclusion of the Talmud and the ruling of the *Tur*. The *Bach* rejects this premise. In his view, careful scrutiny of the Talmudic discussion indicates no differentiation between a "bath" and a "basin" with respect to adding cold water. (Other differentiations, however, are indicated.) He also rejects any differentiation between *Kli Sheni* and *Kli Shelishi*. Whenever a prohibition is applied to a *Kli Sheni*, asserts the *Bach*, it applies equally to any level hot *Kli*. In his view, the *Tur* agrees with *Tosfot*: The Talmudic Bath is a *Kli Sheni* and it is prohibited to add water, to ensure that people do not err because of its great heat, and assume that it is permitted to add cold water to a *Kli Rishon*. For the same reason, concludes the *Bach*, the *Tur* prohibits adding cold water to a basin and to any other vessel used for bathing.[16]

The discussion is incomplete without citing the view of the *Shulchan Arukh* and the *RaMA*. The ruling of the *Shulchan Arukh* is a verbatim quote of the ruling of the *RaMBaM*.[17] Unlike the ruling of the *RaMBaM*, however, the intention of the ruling is clear, due to the common authorship of the *Shulchan Arukh* and the *Kesef Mishneh* commentary on the *RaMBaM*. It can be assumed that the intention of the ruling is as explained in the *Kesef Mishneh*. The bath cited by the *Shulchan Arukh* is a *Kli Rishon*. Accordingly, he would permit adding cold water to a *Kli Sheni* bath.

The *RaMA* disagrees with this ruling. He explicitly prohibits adding cold water to a hot bath "even if it is only a *Kli Sheni*."[18]

In summation: The *Shulchan Arukh*, *Rashi*, the *RaN*, and the *RaMBaM* as interpreted by the *Kesef Mishneh* and the *Lechem Mishneh*, permit pouring cold water into a *Kli Sheni* bath. On the other hand, the *RaMA*, *Tosfot*, the *RaMBaM* as interpeted by the *Bach*'s and *Taz*'s emendation of the *Magid Mishnah*, and the *Tur*, prohibit pouring cold water into a *Kli Sheni* bath. In the latter group, only the *Tur*, according to one approach in the *Beit Yosef* considers it a Torah prohibition. However, no other view in Shabbat laws, Kashrut laws or any other laws for which *Bishul* is important, considers a hot *Kli Sheni* a vessel for which *Bishul* applies.[19] Consequently, the prohibition must be Rabbinic, based upon the great heat of water used for bathing.

This chapter only discussed adding cold water to a hot vessel used for bathing. Two factors remain to be determined.

1. Does the same prohibition apply to pots of food placed into a hot *Kli Sheni*?
2. Does the prohibition of adding water apply to hot water that is not used for bathing?

Chapter 2
Placing Pots of Food into a *Kli Sheni*

Even if it is prohibited to pour cold water into a hot *Kli Sheni* bath, the Talmud indicates that it is permitted to place a receptacle (such as a pot) of cold water into a *Kli Sheni* bath.[20] *Tosfot*, who prohibits adding cold water into a *Kli Sheni* bath, explicitly permits placing a receptacle containing cold water into a *Kli Sheni* bath.[21] Similarly, the language of the *Tur*'s ruling, "the cold water *mixed into them* will be cooked,"[22] implies no prohibition when the cold water is kept separate by an additional receptacle. The *RaMBaM*, as explained by the *Lehem Mishneh* and *Kesef Mishneh*, certainly permits such heating, since he even permits adding cold water into a *Kli Sheni* bath.[23]

On the other hand, the *Magid Mishneh* as emended by the *Bach*[24] and the *TaZ*[25] explains that the bath discussed by the *RaMBaM* is a *Kli Sheni*. As cited in chapter one, the *RaMBaM* prohibits placing a flask of oil into the bath. Since this view considers the bath a *Kli Sheni*, it prohibits placing a flask of oil, and, by extension, any receptacle of liquid into a *Kli Sheni*. Nevertheless, the *Shulchan Arukh* rules that "it is permitted to place a flask of water or of other liquids into a *Kli Sheni* containing hot water"[26] and the *RaMA* indicates agreement by not dissenting with this view. Accordingly, it seems permitted to place a pot of food into a *Kli Sheni* bath.

The basis for this permission can be strengthened in two ways. The first way is to analyze the ruling for placing food directly into a *Kli Sheni*. The *Shulchan Arukh* cites one view that prohibits placing bread into a hot *Kli Sheni* on Shabbat, and the *RaMA* concludes that it is preferable to comply with this view.[27] The *Magen Avraham* explains that some foods are cooked in less heat than others and therefore, would be cooked even in a *Kli Sheni*. He concludes that no food should be placed into a *Kli Sheni* since it may be among those foods cooked in a *Kli Sheni*.[28] Although the *Shulchan Arukh HaRav*, the eighteenth century codification by the founder of the Chabad movement, modifies this ruling to exclude liquids,[29] the *Mishnah B'rurah* implies that liquids may not be placed into a hot *Kli Sheni*.[30]

Nevertheless, the situation changes when dealing with fully cooked food. Fully cooked food, as indicated in Section II, may be reheated on Shabbat. Accordingly, they may certainly be placed into a *Kli Sheni*. Reheating liquids was shown to be the subject of controversy, which may transgress the Torah prohibition of *Bishul*. Yet, even the *Mishnah B'rurah*, who implies that uncooked liquids may not be placed into a *Kli Sheni*, explicitly permits placing cold fully cooked liquids into a *Kli Sheni*.[31]

The second way of strengthening the basis for permission for reheating food in a *Kli Sheni* is by differentiating between a *Kli Sheni* used for bathing, and other *Kli Sheni*. It is only appropriate to state "Because they are for bathing presumably they are very hot" for a *Kli Sheni* used for bathing, not for other purposes. In fact, the Talmud permits pouring cold water into a hot *Kli Sheni* used for drinking.[32] Nevertheless, since the water for reheating food is also "greatly heated", it is difficult to differentiate from a *Kli Sheni* used for bathing.

To summarize: Placing a receptacle of liquid into a *Kli Sheni* seems permitted even according to those who prohibit placing liquid directly into a *Kli Sheni*. As to the general permissibility of placing food into a *Kli Sheni*: Whereas placing uncooked food and liquid into a *Kli Sheni* could be problematic, placing fully cooked food and liquid into a *Kli Sheni* on Shabbat is permitted.

Chapter 3
A Warming Bath for Reheating Food on Shabbat

The previous two chapters have demonstrated that fully cooked food may be heated in a *Kli Sheni* bath on Shabbat. However, the practical implementation of this conclusion is difficult. On one hand, drawing hot water from standard systems to pour into a *Kli Sheni* can transgress the various prohibitions discussed in Section VI. On the other hand, it is impractical, if not impossible, to leave large quanitities of hot water over a covered fire until it is needed.

The solution devised by the Institute for Science and Halakha is as follows: A large boiler automatically transfers hot water into a large bath at preset intervals. At these intervals the bath is drained of its water, thereby maintaining a constant supply of hot water. The bath is kept distinct from the boiler (and thus is a *Kli Sheni*) by positioning the end of the connecting pipe above the water level of the bath. This bath has a constant supply of hot water whose automatic production is independent of any personal Shabbat action (see Section II and VI).

The thermostat of the boiler for this system can be set at a maximum of 90°C. This mitigates the problem of "greatly heated water" discussed in chapter 2. To avoid the problem of *Hatmanah* (see Section I) the warming pots should not be fully immersed in the water. Reheating fully cooked food in this system on Shabbat is permitted.

An alternate permitted method is based upon the automatic Boiler described in Section VI in which water is automatically transferred into a large pot. It is permitted to draw hot water from that vat, as discussed in Section VI, since it does not directly cause *Bishul* of more water. Accordingly, water may be manually transferred from this system into the warming bath when needed. This system has the added advantage of being a *Kli Shelishi* (providing that each vessel is separated from the previous vessel). Consequently, all views but the *Bah* (see Chapter 1) would permit its use. In addition, baked and roasted food, which according to some views cannot be placed into a *Kli Sheni*, could be reheated in a *Kli Shelishi* on Shabbat.[33] Thus, this system can reheat all fully cooked food on Shabbat in a Halakhically permitted manner.

Section III

1. *Shulchan Arukh* Orach Chaim 318:9
2. T.B. Shabbat 42a
3. *Rashi,* Shabbat 42a s.v. Chamin; *Ran al Harif,* Shabbat chapter 3, s.v. *Aval*
4. *Tosfot,* Shabbat 42a s.v. *Aval*
5. *Rambam,* Shabbat Laws 22:5
6. *Magid Mishnah,* Shabbat Laws 22:5
7. *Bach,* Orach Chaim 318
8. *Taz* Orach Chaim 318:18
9. *Kesef Mishneh,* Shabbat Laws 22:5
10. *Lechem Mishneh,* Shabbat Laws 22:5
11. *Tur, Orach Chaim 318*
12. *TB Shabbat 42a*
13. *Beit Yosef,* Orach Chaim 318
14. *Tur,* Orach Chaim 318
15. *Beit Yosef,* Orach Chaim 318. It is also possible to say that the Beit Yosef agrees with the Bach (below) in prohibiting a Kli Shlishi, but this requires forcing the meaning.
16. *Bach,* Orach Chaim 318
17. *Shulchan Arukh,* Orach Chaim 318:11
18. *Rama,* Orach Chaim 318:11
19. More specifically, whereas there is controversy as to whether or not a *Kli Sheni* absorbs, no differentiation is made for a "greatly heated" *Kli Sheni.* Furthermore, the *Shulchan Arukh* and the *Rama* (Yoreh De'ah 105) rule that a *Kli Sheni* does not cook, and even the *Maharshal* cited in the *Taz* (Yoreh De'ah 94:1) who rules that a *Kli Sheni* absorbs, concurs that it does not cook. See *Pri Magadim,* Mishbetzot Zahav Orach Chaim 318:18.
20. TB Shabbat 42a
21. *Tosfot,* Shabbat 42a s.v. Sha'ani
22. *Tur,* Orach Chaim 318
23. As discussed in Chapter one of this section
24. *Bach,* Orach Chaim 318

25. *Taz,* Orach Chaim 318:18
26. *Shulchan Arukh,* Orach Chaim 318:13
27. *Shulchan Arukh* and *Rama,* Orach Chaim 318:5
28. *Magen Avraham,* Orach Chaim 318:18
29. Shulchan Arukh Harav 318:12
30. From the fact that he permits only "milk that has cooled off" in a *Kli Sheni.* See 318:39
31. *Mishnah B'rurah,* Orach Chaim 318:39
32. TB Shabbat 42a
33. *Shulchan Arukh,* Orach Chaim 318:5

SECTION IV

Reheating Food for Hospital Patients

Introduction		111
Chapter 1	*Gerama* of Cooking in a Hospital	113
Chapter 2	Is Hot Metal Considered "Fire?"	117
Chapter 3	The Views of the *Chashmal Le'or HaHalakha* Regarding Whether Hot Metal is Considered Fire	121
Chapter 4	Hot Metal as a "Solar Derivative"	131
Chapter 5	A System for Heating Food on Shabbat for Hospital Patients	137
Chapter 6	An Alternate Solution for Heating Hospital Food	139

Introduction

Many hospitals patients must eat their food at or near their beds. Food cooked in a central kitchen is therefore placed on trays and brought to the patients on a cart. Because of the time lapse until the food reaches the patients, the food often cools off. Medical and taste considerations, however, require serving warm food in hospitals.

Two basic solutions are used in many hospitals to keep the food warm. One solution is to place the carts in warming cabinets in each ward, where the food is reheated. Another solution is to use carts containing heating elements that reheat the food when plugged in. Both of these commonly practiced solutions can involve several transgressions of Shabbat.These transgressions include the cooking related prohibitions such as *Bishul*, *Shehiyah*, *chazarah* and *Nireh Ki-Mevashel*, discussed in Section I, and the prohibitions of *Hav'arah*, *Boneh* and *Molid*, related to the use of the heating element.

To solve the problem of Shabbat, the Institute of Science and Halakha devised two systems based on the existing systems described above. At the heart of both systems is a heating element that does not glow red. The systems are further designed to eliminate any direct human action that would transgress Shabbat prohibitions.

This section analyzes the underlying halakhic principles involved in these solutions. Chapter one discusses the halakhic status of hospitals in general, and specifically the halakhic status of using a pre-set electric time clock to heat food in a hospital warming closet (as opposed to an electric cart) on Shabbat. Chapter two analyzes the prohibition *Hav'arah* and its applicability to heating metal below the point in which it would glow red. Chapter three analyzes the views of the contrary position. Chapter four demonstrates that cooking with the heat of metal that does not glow red, does not transgress the Torah prohibition of *Bishul*. Chapter five describes the technological modifications necessary to permit the Shabbat placement of food into a hospital warming closet activated by a pre-set electric time clock. Chapter six discusses the additional prohibitions involved in electric carts due to the requirement for placing a plug into an outlet on Shabbat. It describes the special Shabbat outlet developed by the Institute to circumvent that problem in a hospital setting.

Chapter 1
Gerama of Cooking in a Hospital

The operation of any food-warming device on Shabbat transgresses the prohibition of *Havarah* when fire, or its equivalent, is produced by human action. Section I discussed the various cooking related prohibitions that are transgressed when food is placed onto a hot surface on Shabbat. Heating food on Shabbat in hospital warming cabinets, (a type of "hot surface") can transgress many of these prohibitions.

These prohibitions could be avoided by leaving food over a covered fire from before the onset of Shabbat. This method, discussed in Section I, is unacceptable in a hospital for medical reasons. Since medically acceptable hot food is nevertheless essential for hospital patients, it is necessary to analyze the circumstances in which food could be warmed in hospitals on Shabbat.

One possible method of warming food on Shabbat, placing food onto a cold area subsequently heated by means of a pre-set electric time-clock, was discussed in Section II. It was indicated that such placement is a *Gerama* of the subsequent heating, and prohibited, as any *Gerama* of a Torah precept is prohibited, unless "harm" (*nezek*) would result from the prohibition. The *Shulchan Arukh HaRav* broadens this ruling and permits *Gerama* of a Torah precept under circumstances of "great need" (*tzorekh gadol*) as well.[1]

One of the categories generally included in the general Halakhic definition of "great need" is mild illness (*mikzat choli*).[2] Every hospital patient is presumably mildly ill at the very least. *Gerama* of cooking for a hospital patient is thus equivalent to *Gerama* of cooking under circumstances of "great need." Since the *Shulchan Arukh HaRav* permits *Gerama* of a Torah precept under circumstances of "great need", he presumably permits Shabbat placement of food for hospital patients into a cold area. Thus, according to the *Shulchan Arukh HaRav*, placing food for hospital patients into a cold warming cabinet subsequently to be heated by means of an electric time clock should be permitted.

This lenient ruling of the *Shulchan Arukh HaRav* is only necessary when a Torah precept is transgressed, if the action is performed in a non-*Gerama* manner. As discussed in the previous sections, reheating fully cooked *dry* food on Shabbat involves no Torah precepts. It was further indicated in Section II that placing fully cooked dry food on Shabbat onto a cold surface that is subsequently heated by means of an electric time clock also need not necessarily involve Rabbinic precepts. Thus, even independent of the lenient ruling of the *Shulchan Arukh HaRav*, placing fully cooked dry food on Shabbat into a cold heating closet that would subsequently be heated by means of an electric time clock could be permitted. (See Section II for the technical modifications required).

But hospital food includes soups and other liquids, the reheating of which involves at least Rabbinic precepts, as discussed in Section II. It was indicated in that section that whereas many authorities permit *Gerama* of a Rabbinic precept, there was evidence that reheating fully cooked liquids involves the transgression of a Torah precept. A *Gerama* of reheating liquids, therefore, which according to this view is a *Gerama* of a Torah precept, would therefore be prohibited, unless the previously presented view of the *Shulchan Arukh HaRav* is accepted.

However, even if the view of the *Shulchan Arukh HaRav* is not accepted, the *Gerama* of a Torah precept in a hospital might nevertheless be permitted. The basis for this lenient ruling involves the Halakhic definition of two other categories of illness, in addition to the previously discussed *mikzat choli*: 1. *choleh She'yesh Bo Sakanah* — a dangerously ill person, and 2. *choleh She'ein Bo Sakanah* — a person whose illness either confines him to bed or afflicts his entire body, although his life is not endangered. All Shabbat precepts may be transgressed to aid a *choleh She'yesh Bo Sakanah*.[3] *Gerama* of cooking, as well as direct cooking, would therefore be permitted for the sake of a *choleh She'yesh Bo Sakanah*.

Unlike the ruling for a *choleh She'yesh Bo Sakanah* no Torah precepts may be transgressed to aid a *choleh She'ein Bo Sakanah*. Certain actions that would otherwise be Rabbinically prohibited may be performed for his benefit, the classic one being the otherwise prohibited action of telling a gentile on Shabbat to cook for a Jew.[4] From the fact that a gentile may be told to do an action for a *choleh She'ein Bo Sakanah*, it can be derived that a Jew can do a *Gerama* of cooking for a *choleh She'ein Bo Sakanah,* although the Halakhic literature does not discuss this point.

The derivation of this point would be as follows: Telling a gentile on Shabbat to cook, or to do any other Shabbat work for a (healthy) Jew is prohibited, regardless of any harm (*nezek*) or loss (*hefsed*) that may result.[5] The prohibition of a Jew doing *Gerama* of Shabbat work seems less stringent, since the *Gerama* is permitted when harm or loss would otherwise result, emphasizing thereby the "weaker" nature of the prohibition of *Gerama*. As indicated above, telling a gentile on Shabbat to cook for a *choleh She'ein Bo Sakanah* is permitted. Since the prohibition of a Jew doing *Gerama* of Shabbat work seems weaker than the prohibition of telling a gentile on Shabbat to do work for a Jew, a Jew should be permitted, a fortiori, (*Kal VaChomer*) to do a *Gerama* of cooking for a *choleh She'ein Bo Sakanah*.

To summarize this point: it has been indicated that Shabbat placement of food into a cold area that will subsequently be heated by means of an electric time clock is a *Gerama* of cooking. It has further been demonstrated that *Gerama* of cooking should be permissable for the sake of a *choleh She'ein Bo Sakanah*. It should therefore be permitted to place hospital food on Shabbat into a cold warming closet (with the minor technical modifications discussed in Section II. Also see Chapter five of this section) that will subsequently be heated by means of an electric time clock, provided that the patients meet the criteria for *choleh She'ein Bo Sakanah..*

Accordingly: If the ruling of the *Shulchan Arukh HaRav* is accepted then the *Gerama* of cooking embodied in placing food onto a cold warming closet that will subsequently be heated by means of an electric time clock is permitted for hospital patients. Without this ruling the situation is somewhat more complicated. If the patients involved are *choleh She'yesh Bo Sakanah*, then this *Gerama*, as well as direct cooking would be permitted for their benefit. If the patients are *choleh*

She'ein Bo Sakanah, then this *Gerama* appears to be permitted as well. If the patients are *Mikzat Choli*, then the permissibility of *Gerama* of cooking for them is dependent upon the type of food involved.

If the type of food involved is fuly cooked dry food, then, since directly reheating fully cooked dry food does not transgress any Torah precepts, the *Gerama* of such cooking is permitted. Placing fully cooked dry food into a cold warming closet (with the technical modifications discussed in Section II to avoid the problem of "stoking") that would subsequently be heated by means of an electric time clock is therefore permitted. If the food is not fully cooked, or not dry, then directly reheating the food could transgress a Torah precept. As a result, *Gerama* of such reheating is prohibited. Since reheating the food in the manner described here involves this prohibited *Gerama*, the food may not be reheated in this manner for patients that are *Mikzat Choli*. The only permitted condition would be if some manner of direct heating of liquids could be found that would at the very least not transgress a Torah prohibition. Under those circumstances, *Gerama* of such heating would be permitted.

Chapter 2
Is Hot Metal Considered "Fire?"

This chapter attempts to prove that directly heating food by means of hot metal that does not glow red transgresses no Torah prohibitions, although it would be Rabbinically proscribed. As discussed in the previous chapter, *Gerama* of such heating should be permitted, since many authorities permit *Gerama* of Rabbinic prohibitions. The lenient situation of a hospital setting was shown to further strengthen this permission.

The basis for proving that directly heating food by means of hot metal that does not glow red transgresses no Torah prohibitions, is the hypothesis that hot metal that does not glow red cannot be considered "fire" or a "fire derivative." *Bishul*, the Torah prohibition normally transgressed when directly heating food on Shabbat, was defined in Section I as cooking that meets certain criteria. One of the criteria of *Bishul* is that the food be heated by fire (*Ur*) or a fire derivative (*Toldot Ha'Ur*). If it can be demonstrated that metal that does not glow red is not considered "fire" or a "fire derivative," then cooking with such metal would not transgress the Torah prohibition of *Bishul*.

The Talmudic discussion concerning the roasting of the Pascal lamb provides convincing evidence that metal that does not glow red cannot be considered fire. The Talmud states:

"If he sliced it [the Pascal lamb] and placed it on embers, Rabi says: I call that 'Roasted by fire.'[6] Rav Ahadvoi Bar Ami asked Rav Hisda: Could Rabi have called embers, 'fire?'... [The answer is] embers of wood need no verse [to prove that they are equivalent to fire in all cases]. Whereas embers of metal need a verse [to prove that they are considered fire for the Pascal lamb]"[7]

Thus, in this case, roasting the Pascal lamb with "embers of metal" meets the Halakhic requirements for "roasted by *fire*,[6]" only because there is an additional verse that specifically includes such heat for roasting the Pascal lamb. By implication, in all other circumstances that require "fire," an "ember of metal" is not considered "fire."

But what is an "ember of metal" (*Gachelet Shel Matekhet*)? Since an ember of wood glows red, does that mean that an "ember of metal" also glows red, and thus differs only with respect to the substance glowing? On the other hand, perhaps an "ember" refers to a substance heated by fire. After wood is heated by fire, it leaves glowing embers. After metal is heated by fire, however, it need not leave glowing "embers."

This question can be brought into sharper focus through demonstrating that where the metal is hot (but at a lower temperature than an ember of metal) it is not considered "fire" even for the Pascal lamb. This can be seen from the Talmudic discussion of the Mishnaic ruling that, "the Pascal Lamb may not be roasted on a (metal) spit nor on a grate:"[8]

The Talmud states:

"Since part of it [the metal] heats up [from contact with the fire] all of it heats up [since metal conducts heat] and it [The Pascal lamb] gets roasted from [contact with] the spit. But the Lord said 'Roasted by fire' and not 'Roasted by other things.'"[9]

Thus, the Talmud does not consider a metal spit that is hot enough to roast meat (but not as hot as an "ember of metal") "fire." If hot metal is not considered "fire" even for the Pascal lamb, then it certainly should not be considered "fire" in other circumstances. "Embers of metal", on the other hand, are considered "fire" for the Pascal lamb only because a special verse includes them in the category of fire.

Thus far, no distinction has been made between glowing and non-glowing metal. The specific inclusion of "metal embers," (as opposed to hot metal) for roasting the Pascal lamb, implies that in absence of such scriptural inclusion, there would be no difference between glowing and non-glowing metal. Evidently, then, even glowing metal would not be considered "fire."

However, to avoid conflict with other sources and authorities who contradict this conclusion,[10] the difference between "embers of metal" and hot metal can be explained as follows: An "ember of metal" refers to exceedingly hot metal that does not of necessity glow red. When it does not glow red, it is not considered "fire," except for roasting the Pascal lamb, for which it is included by a special verse. At the stage in which an "ember of metal" glows red, however, it can be considered fire for all purposes, since it apparently has all the properties of fire. Ordinary hot metal, on the other hand, is less hot than an "ember of metal," and thus is not even included by the verse explaining the Pascal lamb.

It has thus been demonstrated that hot metal that does not glow red cannot be considered "fire." The prohibition of *Bishul* could, however, be transgressed with such heat, if it is considered a "derivative of fire." A "derivative of fire" is any heat whose source is fire, even if there is presently no fire. Cooking with metal that had been heated by fire would thus transgress the prohibition of *Bishul* whether or not the metal glowed, as it would be considered a "fire derivative."

But what of cooking with metal that had been heated by electricity? Electric heat results from the friction caused by electricity forcing its way through a resistor in a heating element. The greater the resistance to the electricity, the greater the friction, and the higher the temperature of the element. When the temperature of the element rises to a given level, the metal of the element glows red. Prior to that point it cannot be considered fire, as demonstrated from the Talmudic discussion concerning the roasting of the Pascal lamb. Since the source for the heat is friction rather than fire, it seems that such heat should not be considered a "fire derivative." Cooking with electric heat in which the metal does not glow red should, therefore, neither be considered "cooking with fire" nor "cooking with a fire derivative." Accordingly, it would seem to transgress no Torah prohibitions.

Chapter 3
The Views of the *Chashmal Le'or HaHalakha* Regarding Whether Hot Metal is Considered Fire

The central thesis of the previous chapter, that non-glowing hot metal is not considered "fire," is contradicted by the *Chashmal Le'or HaHalakha*. The *Chashmal Le'or HaHalakha*, written by the late Rabbi Yudelevitz, is one of the few books to deal in a comprehensive manner with the Halakhic issues concerning electricity. It contains various Talmudic proofs that hot metal should be considered fire even if it does not glow.[11] Since it is one of the few books to grapple with this issue, it is necessary to analyze his proofs, and demonstrate that the sources upon which they are based do not conflict with the conclusions reached in chapter two.

The basis for the first proof of the *Chashmal Le'or HaHalakha*, is the Torah prohibition of *Havarah* on Shabbat which is transgressed when fire is kindled on Shabbat (whether or not anything is cooked). If it can be shown that the Talmud considers a situation *Havarah*, even when the "fire" involved has no flames, nor does it glow, that would indicate that the criteria for "fire" is not dependent upon the presence of flames or glow.

The *Chashmal Le'or HaHalakha* attempts to prove this point by citing the Talmudic discussion of the death sentence *Sereifah*. *Sereifah* was accomplished by pouring molten lead down the throat, so that death results from the scalding of the interior organs.[12] Although no glowing fire is apparently present in *Sereifah*, the Talmud seems to indicate that *Havarah* — and by extension, "fire," — is involved, seemingly supporting the thesis of the *Chashmal Le'or HaHalakha*.

The Talmud analyzes several verses in the Torah:

"[In Exodus it says] 'You shall kindle no fire throughout your habitations [on the day of Shabbat].'¹³ Why did the Torah add '[Throughout] your habitations?' One of Rabbi Yishmael's disciples cites him as saying: Because [in Deuteronomy] it says 'And if a man has committed a capital crime and be put to death.'¹⁴ I would think [that he would be put to death] either during the week or on Shabbat... It therefore has to say [for Shabbat] 'you shall kindle no fire *throughout your habitations*'¹⁵ and it adds [in Numbers] These laws for the regulations of justice [by the courts] shall be unto you for your generations *throughout your habitations.*'¹⁶ Just as 'habitations' here refers to the courts [who regulate justice], 'habitations' there [the Exodus sentence] refers to the courts as well.¹⁷"

Thus, based upon the prohibition for the courts to kindle fire on Shabbat (as derived from "Habitations") the Talmud concludes that the courts may not put a person to death on Shabbat, presumably because "kindling fire" is involved in the death sentence of *Sereifah*.

If so, which part of the process is considered *Havarah*? The original kindling of fire to melt the lead? Melting the lead? Or perhaps scalding the interior organs?

The *Chashmal Le'or HaHalakha* proposes that the *Havarah* involved in the *Sereifah* process is the scalding of the interior organs despite the lack of flame or glow.

He bases this proposal on a passage in the Jerusalem Talmud that stresses that a positive precept should be performed even when its performance involves a negative precept (*Aseh Docheh Lo Ta'aseh*), providing that both occur simultaneously. Furthermore, continues the Jerusalem Talmud, even a transgression of a negative precept that prepares the way for the subsequent performance of a positive precept, could be performed.

However, if that action could generally have been performed previously at a time when no negative precept need have been transgressed, then its performance is not permitted, despite the fact that the subsequent positive precept cannot then be performed.¹⁸ By extension, if the *Havarah* connected to the death penalty refers to the kindling of fire for melting the lead, or to the melting process itself, then both can be performed before Shabbat. As a result, neither could be performed on Shabbat to prepare for the positive precept of putting to death, since both involve negative precepts that can be performed before the onset of Shabbat. Accordingly, a verse to that effect would seemingly be unnecessary. Yet the Jerusalem Talmud says: "And let him be killed on Shabbat? Just as sacrifices which supersede Shabbat are superseded by required [court] killing, as it says, 'From my altar shall you take him to be put to death.'[19] Shabbat which is superseded by sacrifices should certainly be superseded by required [court] killing? Reish Lakish cites Rav Yanai: This teaches that the courts do not judge on Shabbat, as it says [in Exodus] 'you shall kindle no fire throughout your habitations,'[20] and it subsequently says [in Numbers] 'These laws for the regulations of justice shall be unto you for generations throughout your habitations.'[21] Just as there [in Numbers] the verse refers to courts, here [Exodus] too, the verse refers to courts [who may not 'kindle fire' — put to death — on Shabbat]."[22]

Since, as mentioned above a special verse would not be necessary to prohibit preparatory actions that could be performed before Shabbat, and nevertheless a special verse is cited, the *Chashmal Le'or HaHalakha* concludes that this "kindling fire" (*Havarah*) verse prohibits the scalding of the interior organs on Shabbat (which is not a preparatory action). This implies that *Havarah*, and by extension "fire," does not require flames or a glow, and by implication, hot metal that does not glow can also be considered "fire."

This attempted proof assumes that the Jerusalem Talmud is referring to death by burning. It is then appropriate to analyze which part of that death constitutes *Havarah*. But does the Jerusalem Talmud in fact refer to the specific death of burning?

A comparison of the parallel sections in the Jerusalem Talmud and the Babylonian Talmud seems to indicate that the Jerusalem Talmud is referring to all court deaths, not just to the rare case of death by burning. The Babylonian Talmud digressed into the subject of *Havarah* only to discuss the question of whether a positive precept could be performed even when it can only be performed simultaneously with a negative precept of serious penalty (*Aseh Docheh Lo Ta'aseh She'yesh Bo Karet*).[23] Even so, *Tosfot* comments, "'You shall kindle no fire in all your habitations,' cannot possibly apply to [melting] the bar [of lead, since that certainly would not supersede Shabbat because it is only a preparation for the death itself]. Therefore apply it [the verse] to the death itself."[24]

Thus, despite the fact that no part of the actual death process, (as opposed to the preparatory process) involves "kindling fire," *all* putting to death on Shabbat is nevertheless prohibited based on the word "habitations."

The Babylonian Talmud, therefore, which explicitly discusses *Havarah*, can nevertheless be understood as referring to court death in general. Certainly the Jerusalem Talmud, which explicitly discusses general court judgment could also be understood as referring to court death in general. Thus, "You shall kindle no fire..."[20] nevertheless prohibits putting to death on Shabbat, and indeed, even judging on Shabbat, regardless of whether or not "fire" and kindling literally apply. There would be no proof that "fire" applies to a substance that does not glow, and the conclusion of the previous chapter remains valid.

Attempted Proof No. 2

Another attempted proof discussed by the *Chashmal Le'or HaHalakha* is based on the Talmudic and Post-Talmudic rulings concerning the "extinguishing" (*Kibuy*) of a "metal ember" on Shabbat. Since "extinguishing" implies previous fire, whatever state can be "extinguished" would have to be ruled "fire." Thus, if it could be proven that extinction applies to a "metal ember" that does not glow red, that would indicate that hot metal need not glow red to be ruled "fire."

He cites the Talmudic ruling that on Shabbat, "It is permitted to extinguish an ember of metal on public grounds so that the public would not be injured [by contact with the hot metal]; but not to extinguish an ember of wood [which is similarly found on public grounds]."[25]

Thus, the concept "extinction" seemingly applies to an "ember of metal." By extension, an "ember of metal" is seemingly considered "fire." If it can be demonstrated that the "ember of metal" that is considered "fire" is a non-glowing ember, then similarly hot metal could be considered "fire" even if it did not glow red.

To prove this point, the *Chashmal Le'or HaHalakha* cites the commentary of the *Rabeinu Chanan'el*, an early Talmudic commentator of great influence. The citation is cited here at length for subsequent analysis:
"... And extinguishing an ember of metal when it is hot and black and the viewer [passing by] thinks it is cold since it has no redness as would a whispering [wood] ember; and as a result people could be injured by it. It is therefore permitted [to extinguish it]. But an ember of wood; if its redness is gone, it is already extinguished and can cause no injury. And if its redness remains, all who see it avoid it.[26]
The phrase "extinguishing an ember of metal when it is hot and it is black..." seemingly implies that "extinguishing," and thus "fire," applies to an "ember of metal" that is not red hot. Thus, concludes the *Chashmal Le'or HaHalakha*, hot metal that does not glow red can also be considered "fire."

Refutation of the second attempted proof

Careful scrutiny of the above passage, however, could lead to a contrary conclusion as well. A printed note alongside the commentary of *Rabeinu Chanan'el*, in the margins of the standard editions of the Talmud, reads: "For an explanation of the words of *Rabeinu (Chanan'el)* see the *Hidushei HaRaShBA* s.v. 'Gahelet Shel Matekhet.' Examine it carefully."

This *RaShBA* explains why an ember of metal may be extinguished, whereas an ember of wood may not:
"Because an ember of wood is red, and thus seen, it is avoided by passers-by, who will, therefore, not be injured. But [an ember] of metal, is hot and can burn [a passer-by] even when it extinguishes of its own accord. [Since it does not then glow] it would not be seen, and could cause injury. These are the words of *Rabeinu Hai Gaon*, as well as [the intention] of the author of the *Halakhot (Gedolot)* and *Rabeinu Chanan'el*."[27]

According to the *RaShBA*, therefore, *Rabeinu Chanan'el* permits extinguishing a red-hot metal ember to cool it, and thereby prevent public injury. Otherwise, the ember would gradually extinguish of its own accord, while remaining in a state in which it is "hot and it would burn, and it would not be seen, and could cause injury." Most important, for our purposes, is the fact that *Rabeinu Chanan'el*, as cited by the *RaShBA*, considers a hot ember that "would burn and would not be seen," "extinguished." If it is "extinguished," then it cannot be considered "fire," and only a glowing ember could be considered "fire." Yet, the interpretation of the *RaShBA* is challenged by the explicit words of the *Rabeinu Chanan'el*: "*Extinguishing* an ember of metal when it is hot *and it is black*..." How then can the *RaShBA* call a hot black ember "extinguished?" Furthermore, how can this interpretation be called the view of *Rabeinu Chanan'el* himself?

The question can be answered by noting that *Rabeinu Chanan'el*'s commentary, (as well as most commentaries up to modern times) was written with no punctuation. Without punctuation, *Rabeinu Chanan'el* is understood as saying that a "hot black ember" can be "extinguished," and by extension, that non-glowing metal could be considered "fire." The *RaShBA*, however, is telling us, in effect, to add a colon after the word "metal" in the explanation of *Rabeinu Chanan'el*, thereby transforming the first phrase into an introductory phrase. The explanation would then read:

..."And extinguishing an ember of metal:
When it is hot and it is black [i.e. when the metal ember is self-extinguished], the viewer [passing by] thinks that is cold, since it has no redness as would a whispering [wood] ember; and as a result, people could be injured by it. It is therefore permitted [to extinguish the red hot ember of metal, so that it may be cooled in the process of extinction, and thus, no one would be injured]."[26]

If the first phrase is an introductory phrase, then *Rabeinu Chanan'el* considers a metal ember that no longer glows red "extinguished." Extinguishing a glowing metal ember, which is normally equivalent to extinguishing fire, is nevertheless permitted when it is on public grounds. The reason for this permission is to prevent the danger to the passer-by of being burnt by very hot metal that no longer glows and therefore appears cool.

Thus, the attempted proof of the *Chashmal Le'or HaHalakha*, based on an apparently straightforward interpretation of *Rabeinu Chanan'el*, is incompatible with the interpretation given by the

RaShBA. Since the interpretations of the Rishonim are generally accepted as more valid than later interpretations for understanding *Rabeinu Chanan'el*, the interpretation presented here seems more valid than the interpretation of the *Chashmal Le'or HaHalakha*. Accordingly, only metal that glows can be considered "fire," and when metal does not glow it is "extinguished" and thus, no longer "fire."

The Third Attempted Proof

The *Chashmal Le'or HaHalakha* cites the *RaMBaN*, another authority of the Rishonim period, as additional proof that hot metal that does not glow could be considered "fire." The *RaMBaN* asks how the Talmud can rule that placing hot lumps of wrought iron (apparently similar to an "ember of metal") into cold water transgresses a Rabbinic prohibition,[28] if extinguishing a metal ember normally transgresses a Torah prohibition? His answer:
"Perhaps lumps of wrought-iron are not hardened (in cold water) — (*tziruf*) — as a (metal) ember would be, since they are exceedingly hot and they heat the water. Proper hardening can only occur in cold water."[29]

"Hardening metal" introduces a complicating factor to the previous discussion on extinguishing a metal ember. According to the *RaMBaN*, "hardening" seems to be the determining factor for the Torah prohibition, and when "hardening" occurs, a Torah prohibition is transgressed, whether or not the metal is red hot. By contrast, his contemporary, the *Tosfot Yeshanim* answers the same question by saying that the Torah prohibition applies to red hot metal (embers), whereas the Rabbinic prohibition applies to non-red hot metal (lumps of wrought iron).[30] The fact that the *RaMBaN* does not answer in this more direct fashion, is used by the *Chashmal Le'or HaHalakha* to prove that according to the *RaMBaN* there is no difference between red hot and non red hot metal. Since there is no difference between the two according to the *RaMBaN*, and both are considered "fire," he had to differentiate on the basis of "hardening." Thus, concludes the *Chashmal Le'or HaHalakha*, hot metal that does not glow red can be considered "fire."

Refutation of the Third Attempted Proof

Several objections can be raised against this attempted proof. First, the *RaMBaN* need not consider either "metal embers" or lumps of wrought iron "fire." His only concern is whether or not "hardening" takes place, *regardless* of whether or not "fire" was "extinguished." In his view, when metal is hardened, a Torah prohibition is transgressed. Thus, the presence or absence of "fire" could be irrelevant.

Second, the phrase "Since they are exceedingly hot" implies that the wrought iron is hotter than ordinary hot metal (whether or not is is as hot as "embers"). If the *RaMBaN* assumes that the wrought iron is hotter than ordinary hot metal, then that would preclude saying that the iron, unlike the embers, is not red hot. "Exceedingly hot" need not be red hot, but it is difficult to say that it could *never* be red hot. Thus the *RaMBaN*, unlike the *Tosfot Yeshanim*, cannot explain that embers are red hot whereas wrought iron is not red hot. The fact that the *RaMBaN* did not differentiate between "metal embers" and wrought iron can therefore, not be cited as proof that hot metal that does not glow red is considered "fire."

Fourth Attempted Proof

A similar attempted proof by the *Chashmal Le'or HaHalakha* is based upon the *RaMBaM* who rules that "heating iron in order to harden it in water is a subcategory of *Havarah* and is [a Torah prohibition of Shabbat]"[31] The fact that the *RaMBaM* does not write "heating iron *until it is red hot*"... is taken by the *Chashmal Le'or HaHalakha* as proof that the *RaMBaM* applies the prohibition of *Havarah* even if the metal does not glow red.

Refutation of the Fourth Attempted Proof

The very next ruling of the *RaMBaM* seems to refute this proof. He asserts:
"Extinguishing a metal ember is not a Torah prohibition, unless done in a manner of 'hardening' [since] that is the manner of blacksmiths. They heat the iron until it becomes an ember and they extinguish it in

water to harden it. That is *tziruf*, a Torah prohibition that is a subcategory of extinction."³²

Just as the reference to blacksmiths implies that the ember to be extinguished (and hardened) is red hot, (since the metal used by blacksmiths is red hot), so too the previous ruling, "Heating iron to harden it in water," presumably refers to red hot iron. Thus, only when it is red hot would metal be considered "fire" for *Havarah,* extinction, or any other purpose. The attempted proof of the *Chashmal Le'or HaHalakha,* therefore, does not apply.

In summation: The various attempted proofs of the *Chashmal Le'or HaHalakha* have been presented. Each of the attempts was refuted through careful analysis of the sources. The refutations have underscored the premise that metal that does glow red may be considered "fire," whereas metal that does not glow red could not be considered "fire."³³

Chapter 4
Hot Metal as a "Solar Derivative"

The previous two chapters have demonstrated that hot metal that does not glow red is not considered fire. It was also indicated in Chapter 2 that metal heated as a result of electrical resistance cannot be considered a "fire derivative." If it can be considered neither "fire" nor "fire derivative," then what can it be considered?

In addition to the above-mentioned categories of fire and fire derivatives, two additional categories are discussed in the Halakhic literature: Sun and sun-derivatives. Cooking with direct solar heat on Shabbat is permitted, whereas cooking with heat-derived from the sun is Rabbinically proscribed due to its similarity to cooking with heat derived from fire.[34]

Superficially, metal heated by electrical resistance is apparently neither in the category of direct solar cooking nor in the category of solar derivatives, since the heat is clearly not derived from the sun. Yet, there are several other examples of heat from non-fire and non solar sources that the Talmud considers "derivatives of the sun."

One of these examples is based upon the Mishnaic ruling that an egg "may not be roasted by burying it in [hot] sand or road dust."[35] The Talmud explains that hot "road dust" is a solar derivative.[36] Yet, one of the definitions given for "road dust" is dust heated as a result of the friction created by wagon wheels passing over.[37] Thus, heat resulting from non-fire, non-solar sources, in this case friction, can be considered a "solar derivative."[37a]

Another example is based on the example of the Tiberias Hot Springs. The Tiberias Hot Springs are considered "solar derivatives" despite the fact that their heat is not derived from the sun.[38] Thus, the category of "solar derivative" can seemingly also include non-fire related heat sources and, by extension, perhaps include metal heated as a result of the friction produced by electrical resistance.

Since, as previously mentioned, cooking with a solar derivative does not transgress a Torah prohibition, cooking with metal heated as a result of electrical resistance, presumably a solar derivative, also should not transgress a Torah prohibition. On the other hand, perhaps the general category of solar derivative is exempted from a Torah prohibition because of a reason that does not relate to metal heated by electrical resistance. It is, therefore, necessary to discuss the reason why cooking with a solar derivative does not transgress a Torah prohibition, and analyze the applicability of the reasons to metal heated by electrical resistance.

The first reason is that of *Rashi*. *Rashi* explains that no Torah prohibition is transgressed by solar heat (and its derivatives), because such cooking "is not in the normal manner of cooking."[39] This seems to base the exemption from the Torah prohibition on whether or not it is the "normal manner of cooking." Thus, if it would be the "normal manner of cooking" to cook with a solar derivative, then it would evidently be prohibited. Thus, because cooking in an electric oven, is a normal manner of cooking, regardless of whether or not the elements are red hot, it would seem to transgress a Torah prohibition, according to *Rashi*.[40]

Notwithstanding this conclusion, it is impossible to interpret *Rashi* in this manner. The first reason that it is impossible, is based upon a comparison of the Talmudic case of cooking in a solar derivative to the Talmudic case of cooking in a fire derivative. The Talmudic case of cooking in a solar derivitave is cooking a substance by wrapping it in cloths heated by the sun. Similarly, the Talmudic case of cooking in a fire derivative is cooking a substance by wrapping it in cloths heated by fire.[41] Clearly it is no more the "normal manner of cooking" to cook in cloths heated by fire, than to cook in cloths heated to an equal temperature by the sun. Nevertheless, cooking with cloths heated by fire transgressed a Torah prohibition, whereas cooking with cloths heated by the sun does not. Thus, factors other than "normal manner of cooking" must be involved, and *Rashi* cannot be understood in this manner.

The second reason that *Rashi* cannot be interpreted in that manner is based upon the Talmudic controversy concerning the status of the Tiberias Hot Springs. The Talmud's analysis of the Tiberias Hot Springs raises the question of whether or not the springs are in fact heated by means of internal fire.[42] If the prohibitory factor were the "normal manner of cooking," it should merely be necessary to determine whether or not the springs are normally used for cooking. Since the Talmudic controversy does not revolve around this point, it seems that factors other than "the normal manner of cooking," are involved.

The third reason that *Rashi* cannot be interpreted in that manner is based upon the concept of *Kil'achar Yad*, the performance of a prohibited action in a non-normal (irregular) manner. Whereas regarding Shabbat laws performing a prohibited action in an irregular manner does not transgress a Torah prohibition, (though it would transgress a Rabbinic prohibition), regarding laws not related to Shabbat such performance does transgress a Torah prohibition.[43] Thus, even if cooking in non-fire related sources is not considered "cooking" by the Torah for Shabbat because it is not "the normal manner" (i.e. *Kil'achar Yad*) such cooking should nevertheless be considered "cooking" by the Torah for all other laws.

Yet, the Talmud rules that eating a Paschal Lamb cooked in the Tiberias Hot Springs would not transgress the injunction "you may not eat of it... cooked in water,"[44] implying that it is not considered "cooked."[45] Furthermore, the Talmud does not consider blood or *Cheilev* (the prohibited part of an animal's abdominal fat) cooked by the sun as Halakhically "cooked."[46]

Since "the normal manner of cooking" applies only to Shabbat laws and, nevertheless, these non-Shabbat examples are to be considered "uncooked" the reason must be some factor other than the "normal manner of cooking."

Notwithstanding all the reasons why *Rashi* cannot mean the "normal manner of cooking," he explicitly states the reason being that "it is not the normal manner of cooking." Because of the authoritative nature of *Rashi*, and because *Rashi* was not contested by the other Rishonim, it is imperative to find a manner of interpreting *Rashi* that avoids the above questions.

The *Eglei Tal*, a major nineteenth century work on the laws of

Shabbat, interprets *Rashi* in a manner that answers the quesions raised above. He explains that when *Rashi* refers to "not the normal manner of cooking" he refers to a difference in the food itself, not to a difference in the manner of performance. One of the classic cases of *Kil'achar Yad*, writing with the left hand on Shabbat, illustrates this distinction. Writing with the left hand on Shabbat is not the normal manner of writing and being *Kil'achar Yad*, it transgresses no Torah prohibitions. Nevertheless, everything about a letter written with the left hand can be identical to a letter written with the right hand. Since the *result* of the writing by *Kil'achar Yad* is equivalent to writing normally, it is Rabbinically proscribed on Shabbat, and could be considered "writing" any other time. This type of *Kil'achar Yad*, however, does not apply to food cooked in a non-fire related heat, since the result of food cooked in non-fire related heat, according to the *Eglei Tal,* is not equivalent to the result of food cooked in fire related heat. It is therefore considered by the Torah as if it did not "cook", both for Shabbat (when it may be Rabbinically proscribed) and for other precepts.

But in what way is the result of food cooked in non-fire related heat different from the result of food cooked in fire-related heat? The *Eglai Tal* postulates a "fire factor" present in food cooked in fire related heat and absent in all other food. He bases this on the Talmudic concept that the "taste of the wood (fire) improves the taste of the bread," (*Yesh Shevah Etzim BePat*)[47] This "fire factor," whether or not it can be measured, affects the food to the degree that when it is absent the resulting food is not considered cooked through "the normal manner of cooking."[48]

To be considered "cooked" by the Torah, therefore, fire must be used. This would seem to be the intention of the *Piskei RID*, of the Rishonim era, who comments on the Talmudic passage "With sun all agree that it [cooking] is permitted."[42] He explains: "It is inappropriate to prohibit the sun because of [a preventive measure against mistakenly permitting] fire, since *cooking in the sun is not considered cooking.*"[49] Thus, the sun may in fact "cook" but that "is not considered cooking." The *Meiri*, another Rishon, writes similarly "the sun is not included in the category of cooking."[50] By extension, a derivative of the sun can "cook" no more than the sun itself.

Nevertheless, a solar derivative is Rabbinically prohibited on Shabbat, because of its apparent similarity to a fire derivative.

According to the *Eglei Tal*'s interpretation of *Rashi*, cooking food with a solar derivative transgresses no Torah prohibitions because it lacks the fire factor. Similarly, if, as indicated above, metal heated by electrical resistance to less than red hot is a solar derivative and also lacks the fire factor, then cooking with such heat would not transgress a Torah prohibition.

The *Kiryat Sefer*, a commentary on Maimonides of the early Acharonim period, provides an additional explanation why the Torah prohibits cooking on Shabbat with fire and its derivatives only: Cooking would only be with fire and its derivatives, since it was that way also with the dyes cooked for the Tabernacle.[51] Since "the dyes cooked for the Tabernacle" (the archetype for examples of Shabbat work. See General Introduction) were cooked only with fire, cooking with metal heated less than red hot by electrical resistance would seemingly not transgress any Torah prohibitions.[52]

To summarize: It has been demonstrated that heat resulting from electrical resistance is considered a solar derivative, unless the metal glows red. It was also indicated that cooking with a solar derivative on Shabbat does not transgress the Torah prohibition of cooking on Shabbat. Two reasons were given for this; that of *Rashi* and that of the *Kiryat Sefer*. *Rashi*, as interpreted by the *Eglei Tal* and supported by other commentaries, shows that the lack of the "fire factor" eliminates the Torah prohibition of cooking. Electrically heated metal that does not glow red also lacks the "fire factor" and cooking with such heat on Shabbat should therefore not transgress a Torah prohibition. The *Kiryat Sefer* exempts food cooked on Shabbat in a solar derivative from the Torah prohibition, because it was not the method of cooking used during the erection of the Tabernacle. Thus, cooking on Shabbat with electrically heated metal that does not glow red should also not transgress a Torah prohibition.[53]

Chapter 5
A System for Heating Food on Shabbat for Hospital Patients

The previous chapters have developed the Halakhic basis for a system that can heat cold food on Shabbat for hospital patients. Chapter one indicated that placing food on Shabbat onto a cold surface that would subsequently be heated by means of an electrical time clock is considered a *Gerama* of the subsequent cooking. It was indicated there that many authorities permit the performance of a *Gerama* of a Rabbinic prohibition in general and specifically for hospital patients. Chapters 2, 3 and 4 demonstrated that cooking with electrically heated metal that does not glow red is a Rabbinic prohibition. Thus, placing food on Shabbat onto a cold surface such as a heating cabinet that would subsequently be heated by means of an electric time clock should be permitted in a hospital setting, provided that the heating elements do not glow red. To further mitigate any Halakhic problems, fully cooked frozen food should be used, as discussed in Chapter 1.

Nevertheless, several problems remain. The first problem is the technical problem of designing a heating element that does not glow red. This can be solved by using an exposed central element in conjunction with a fan large enough to disperse the air throughout the cabinet, as is the case in a standard convection oven. The rapid dispersal of the heat prevents the element from glowing red. It is, of course, necessary to insure that the fan operates whenever the element does.

A more technical solution is based upon the temperature at which metal glows. This important Halakhic point was determined in a recent NATO study related to the glowing of missiles at night. If a margin of safety is added to their results to ensure that glow (and thus fire) does not result on Shabbat, the metal may be heated to 400°C.[54] Generally speaking, lengthening a given heating element will reduce the power density in watts per unit of length or area. The temperature of the heating element would thus be reduced, as would its tendency to glow.

A second problem was discussed in section II. If the Halakhic problem of "stoking the coals" (see section I) is equivalent to adjusting the temperature, then the cabinet must be designed to eliminate the possibility of temperature adjustment or interfering in any way with the the heating process. This can be accomplished by placing the controls inside the cabinet and designing an electro-magnetic lock that is activated (and locked) whenever the cabinet is being heated.

This type of lock also prevents hospital workers from placing food into a hot cabinet which would be direct action, not *Gerama*. To make this system easier to use a timer could start a bell ringing, which can serve as a warning that the termination of the permitted food placing period is approaching. A few minutes later, the heat and the electromagnetic lock are activated.

Thus, to permit the preparation of heated food on Shabbat in a hospital, we have the following lenient factors:

1. Fully cooked frozen food, which eliminates the Torah prohibition of *Bishul* with respect to the non-liquid food,
2. A heating element that does not glow red, to avoid the Torah prohibitions of *Bishul* and *Havarah*,
3. A time clock to activate the cabinet after food placement, so that the placement be considered a *Gerama* of a Rabbinic prohibition,
4. A hospital setting, to strengthen the permissibility of this *Gerama* of a Rabbinic prohibition, and technical modifications; including placing the controls inside the cabinet and an electro-magnetic lock, to prevent the possibility of temperature adjustment and the possibility of placing food into a warm cabinet.

Chapter 6
An Alternate Solution for Heating Hospital Food

The solution described in the previous chapter assumes that a given hospital owns many food warming cabinets that can be modified in the manner described above. Yet, many hospitals bring the foods to the wards on electric carts containing their own heating elements that warm the food when plugged into the outlets of each ward. This introduces a problem in addition to those solved in the previous chapter: The problem of closing an electric circuit.

Closing an electric circuit on Shabbat is considered by many a transgression of the Rabbinic prohibition *Molid*, literally "begetting," which refers to producing an actual entity out of a potential entity.[55] An example of this, is stirring an ice cube to melt it. The production of actual water from the "potential water" (ie. the ice cube) involves *Molid*. In this case, the production of actual electric current by closing the circuit is viewed as *Molid*.

Since *Molid* is a Rabbinic prohibition, the solutions described in the previous chapter are applicable. Thus, if closing a circuit involves the Rabbinic precept of *Molid*, then an electric time clock could be used to ensure that no current flows in the outlet when the plug is placed into the outlet. The plug placement does not then close any electric circuits, and merely fuctions as a *Gerama* (see Chapter 1) of the subsequent closing of the circuit when the time clock re-allows the current to flow. Since this is a *Gerama* of a Rabbinic prohibition in a hospital setting, it should be permitted, as indicated above.

The *Chazon Ish* however, considers the closing of an electric circuit on Shabbat a transgression of the Torah prohibition *Boneh* (building). In his view, closing a circuit allows current to transform a non-functioning mass of metal into a functioning electric unit, thereby "building" the unit.⁵⁶ Accordingly, placing the plug into the outlet when an electric time clock ensures that no current flows should be Rabbinically prohibited, since it is a *Gerama* of a Torah prohibition.

A differentiation can be made, however, between plugging in an electric food cart and normally closing a circuit. Unlike a normal circuit, the electric food cart is designed to be moved from ward to ward, in each of which it is temporarily plugged in. Since it is designed to repeatedly be "built" and "destroyed", it is never considered completely "built." The *Chazon Ish* considers even such *Boneh* a transgression of the Torah prohibition, but seemingly only when there is electrical current in the outlet. When current flows in the socket, placing the plug effects an electrical connection that could be considered *Boneh*. When no current flows at the time of placement, however, the mechanical connection effected could be considered *Rafuy*, a weak temporary connection that does not involve a Torah prohibition.⁵⁷

Nevertheless, even if a Torah prohibition is not involved, a Rabbinic prohibition could be involved. The view of the *Chazon Ish* therefore, seemingly precludes use of any system that must be plugged in on Shabbat.

The Institute for Science and Halakha developed a "Shabbat outlet" for use in extenuating circumstances (such as in hospitals) that would avoid the problems raised by this view of the *Chazon Ish*. At the heart of this outlet is a "Gerama circuit" based upon the Halakhic principle of *Meniat Hameniah* ("preventing the preventor"). This principle may be illustrated with a water analogy. Supposing some device is activated when water from the overflow of a constantly filling vessel falls upon it. If this vessel would have a spigot that is periodically opened, then the water would never overflow, and the device would never be activated. Preventing the opening of the spigot, "prevents" the escape of water which had prevented the overflow of water that activated the device. As a result, the device is activated. The direct cause of the activation is the water, which flowed from before Shabbat and is therefore unconnected to prohibited Shabbat action. Preventing the opening of the spigot allows the water to do what it was hitherto prevented from doing, but this is only an indirect *Gerama* of the subsequent activation.⁵⁸

The Shabbat outlet functions in a similar, (though more technically complex) manner. Instead of overflowing water activating a device, a fully charged capacitor powers an activating relay which closes the contact that activates the outlet. Just as a spigot prevented the water from overflowing, the capacitor is prevented from building its charge up to the voltage level necessary to activate the relay. The technical manner of accomplishing this is by means of a repetitive periodic impulse of voltage, several milliseconds in length, that is transmitted every few seconds to the light source of a photoelectric device. The photoelectric eye receiving this light impulse from the light source, transmits it electronically to the capacitor which is discharged by these light impulses. Thus, the outlet could never be activated. If the pulses are prevented from reaching the capacitor, the capacitor is not prevented from activating the outlet. This can be accomplished by designing the outlet so that the lip of an extra prong would block the photo-electric impulses. A five prong plug, such as is used for three phase electricity, is easily adaptable for this purpose. (Figure 4.1)

Thus, the problem raised by the view of the *Chazon Ish* is avoided. The connection normally prohibited by the *Chazon Ish* is the initial contact of the prongs with the outlet contacts, enabling current to flow. In this case, that connection does not, and never will, allow current to flow. Only after the subsequent mechanical (as opposed to electrical) pushing into the outlet would the tip of the extra prong block the photo-electric impulses from discharging the capacitor. That extra pushing closes no additional circuits, nor does it newly connect an appliance to an area in which current will subsequently flow. It merely inserts a mechanical barrier between the light source and the photoelectric eye.

This can be further compared to the lenient ruling for closing a window that prevents wind from extinguishing a candle.⁵⁹ The extra prong which prevents the impulses from discharging the capacitor is comparable to the window which prevents the wind from extinguishing the fire.⁶⁰ Indeed, whereas the wind is present at the time the window is closed, each impulse is a discrete unit that is not yet in existence at the time that the plug is placed into the outlet. This is so far removed from

GRAMMA OUTLET

* Is activated by a "GRAMMA" arrangement
* Is based upon photo-electric operation
* Electrical supply to the outlet is single phase 10 amps
* The outlet and plug structure is the three phase type
* An electrically unutilized prong of the plug blocks reception of light rays by the photo-electric cell (sensor)

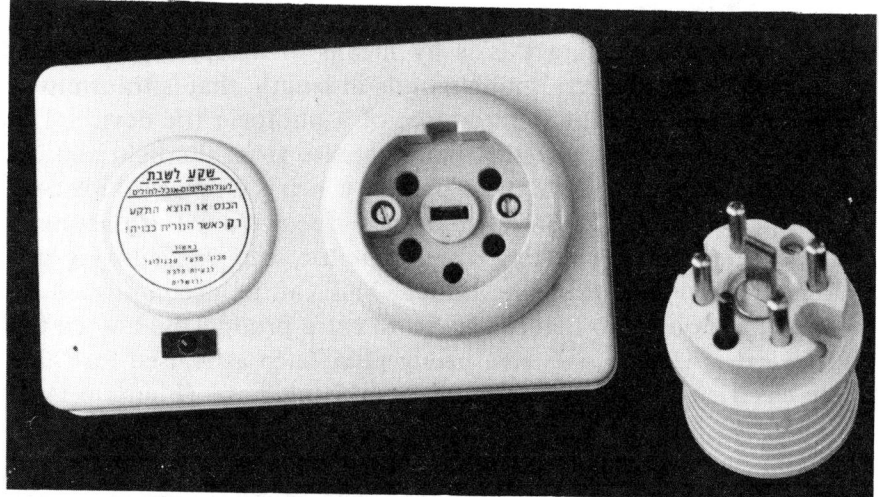

Fig. 4.1

DESCRIPTION OF OPERATION

1. A light emitting diode (LED) lights on and off at predetermined cyclic intervals.
2. It is *permissible* to plug in or out *only* when the red LED is *not lit* (about ½ minute).
3. It is *forbidden* to plug in or out when the red LED *is lit* (about 2 minutes).
4. When plugging in, one of the prongs of the plug blocks reception of light rays in a photoelectric Gramma switch.
5. After a delay, via a Gramma activation, and only when the lamp is lit the next time will the outlet be powered, so that the cart heating can begin.
6. Cart heating will last about 2 minutes, and will be interrupted for about ½ minute, intermittently, as long as the plug is in the outlet.
7. When the lamp goes out, while the plug is still in the outlet, the power to the outlet is interrupted, and a buzzer will sound for about 2 seconds.
8. The buzzer indicates the beginning of the period when it is permissible to pull the plug out of the outlet.
9. It is permissible to pull the plug out *only* when the lamp is *not lit* (about ½ minute).

forbidden action (*Ma'aseh* — see section II, Chapter 1) that it should be considered at most a *Gerama*.

In addition, a timer should periodically de-activate the outlet, and the plug should only be connected at those times. Then, the *Gerama* is a *Gerama* of a Rabbinic prohibition, and thus permitted at least in a hosptial setting. The on and off periods should be of short durtion with indication lights, to enhance the likelihood that the instructions to plug or unplug only during periods in which there is no voltage are followed. Where possible, it is preferable to design an electromagnetic lock to grasp the plug or close the empty outlet whenever there is voltage.

Electric food carts could then be plugged into such outlets on Shabbat to warm food for hospital patients. Needless to say, the requirements discussed in the previous chapter, such as heating elements that do not glow red, are required for this system as well, for the reasons cited in the previous chapter.

Thus, either of the two systems are permitted because they involve a *Gerama* of a Rabbinic prohibition in a hospital setting. The additional problem of closing a circuit, raised by the system described in this chapter, has been solved through use of the Shabbat outlet. If the reason for the prohibition of closing an electric circuit is *Molid* then using the Shabbat outlet involves — at most — a *Gerama* of a Rabbinic prohibition in a hospital setting. If the reason for the prohibition is *Boneh* then using the Shabbat outlet also involves — at most — a *Gerama* of a Rabbinic prohibition, since the Torah prohibition is removed by placing this type of plug into the outlet when there is no voltage. In any case, it should be permitted to use such carts for hospital patients.[61]

Section IV

1. *Shulchan Arukh HaRav,* Orach Chaim 265, 514; *Kuntres Acharon* 3
2. *Shulchan Arukh* Orach Chaim 307:5
3. *Shulchan Arukh,* Orach Chaim 328:2
4. *Shulchan Arukh,* Orach Chaim 328:17
5. *Shulchan Arukh,* Orach Chaim 307:2, 5
6. *Exodus* 12:8
7. TB Pesachim 75a
8. *Pesachim* 7:2
9. TB Pesachim 74a
10. *Rambam* Shabbat Laws 12:1, and commentary of *Magid Mishnah.* Also see on.
11. *Chashmal Le'or HaHalakha* Section I
12. TB Sanhedrin 52a. This preserves the dignity of the human body while killing instantly.
13. *Exodus* 35:3
14. *Deuteronomy* 21:22
15. *Exodus* 35:3
16. *Numbers* 35:29
17. TB Yevamot 6b
18. TJ Pesahim 3:5 at end with commentaries of *Korban Ha'Edah* and *P'nei Mosheh*
19. *Exodus* 21:14
20. *Exodus* 35:3
21. *Numbers* 35:29
22. TJ Sanhedrin 4:6
23. TB Yevamot 6b
24. *Tosfot,* Yevamot 6b s.v. *Ta'ama,* in the margin
25. TB Shabbat 42a
26. *Rabeinu Chanan'el* Shabbat 42a
27. *Chidushei HaRashba,* Shabbat 42a s.v. *Gahelet* also see *Ran Al Harif,* Shabbat III s.v. *Meha*
28. TB Yoma 34b
29. *Hidushei HaRamban,* Shabbat 42a s.v. *Mekhabin*

30. *Tosfot Yeshanim*, Shabbat 35b s.v. *"Hani mili"*
31. *Rambam* Shabbat Laws 12:1
32. *Rambam* Shabbat Laws 12:2, also see *Magid Mishnah* on 12:1
33. This is consistant with the *Magid Mishnah* Shabbat Laws 12:1 who says "Since it becomes light and it burns it is like fire"
34. *Shulchan Arukh,* Orach Chaim 318:3; TB Shabbat 39a; *Rambam,* Shabbat Laws 9:3
35. *Shabbat* 3:3
36. TB Shabbat 38b
37. *Shvitat HaShabat* M'lekhet Mevashel 17 and the notes of the *Be'er Rechovot* 45
37A. See *Tiferet Yisra'el* Shabbat 3:3
38. TB Shabbat 39a. Even the view that considers it a fire derivative explains that that is only because the fires of Gehenna heat it. By implication, were that not the case, they too agree that it is a solar derivative.
39. *Rashi* Shabbat 39a s.v. "De'Shari"
40. This is the conclusion of *Igrot Mosheh,* Orach Chaim Volume 3:52
41. TB Shabbat 39a
42. *ibid.*
43. Only for Shabbat is *"M'lekhet Machshevet"* necessary for prohibition
44. *Exodus* 12:9
45. TB Pesachim 41b
46. TB Menachot 21a
47. TB Pesachim 27a
48. *Eglei Tal* M'lekhet Ha'ofeh 44
49. *Piskei Rid* Shabbat 39a
50. Hidushei Ha'Meiri Shabbat 38b in his explanation of the Mishnah.
51. The *Kiryat Sefer* does not give *Rashi's* explanation because he understood the *Rambam* in Forbidden Foods 9:6 as considering Tiberias springs possible Torah cooking
52. *Kiryat Sefer*, Shabbat Laws 9:2 & 3
53. A microwave oven also cooks without fire or metal that gets red hot, and would thus be as discussed here. But see *Igrot Mosheh*, Orach Chaim III:52 for a different approach
54. Nato study cited in HaMachone number 22
55. *Shu't Beit Yizhak* Yoreh De'ah Volume II, Index 31
56. *Chazon Ish,* Orach Chaim 53
57. See *Chazon Ish*, Orach Chaim 53:9 and the letter of the *Chazon Ish* to Rabbi Auerbach cited on page 19 of his *"Kovetz Ma'amarim B'Inyanei Chashmal Be'Shabbat"*

58. See *Ma'aseh U'Gerama Ba'Halakha* 4:13
59. TB Shabbat 120b; *Shulchan Arukh* and *Rama,* Orach Chaim 277:1
60. According to *Tosfot* Shabbat 120b s.v. *Pote'ach* closing the window allows *Havarah* to result when the flame grows. See Ma'aseh u'Gerama Bahalakhah, Part IV:13
61. Nevertheless, the first method is Halakhically preferable.

SECTION V

The Thermostat in Refrigeration and Heating

Introduction		149
Chapter 1	Thermostatic Systems	151
Chapter 2	Affecting the Thermostat and *Pesik Reisha*	153
Chapter 3	Actions that Lengthen an Existing Status	157
Chapter 4	Conclusion	159

Introduction

The thermostat is at the heart of most modern heating and refrigeration systems. It maintains the temperature within predetermined limits by perceiving temperature changes and affecting the mechanism accordingly. For example, if the temperature rises above a certain point in a refrigerator, or falls below a certain point in a heater, the thermostat activates a refrigeration mechanism or a heating mechanism. Conversely, if the temperature falls beneath a certain point in a refrigerator, or rises above a certain point in a heater, the thermostat de-activates the refrigeration mechanism or the heating mechanism.

Among the factors that can affect the temperature perceived by the thermostat are human actions. These include opening or closing the door that separates the unit from room temperature, placing food into the unit that is of a different temperature from the temperature of the unit, and other actions. Since these actions change the temperature, it can cause the thermostat to activate or de-activate the mechanism that equalizes the temperature. Directly activating or de-activating mechanisms on Shabbat transgresses various prohibitions. Consequently, a question arises: Under what circumstances may the temperature in refrigeration or heating devices be affected by human interference on Shabbat without transgressing any prohibitions of Shabbat?

Chapter one explains how the thermostat works, and describes various common systems in which it is used. Chapter two analyzes the problems of affecting the temperature when the mechanism will be activated or de-activated as a result of the temperature change. Chapter three discusses affecting the temperature when the mechanism will not be activated or de-activated as a result of the temperature change, but will stay active or inactive longer. Chapter four applies the conclusions of chapters two and three to the systems described in chapter one, and describes alternatives to the thermostat to avoid the problems discussed.

Chapter 1
Thermostatic Systems

The thermostat is based upon the principle that most metals expand when their temperature increases, and contract when their temperature decreases. Different metals expand and contract at different rates. Accordingly, if two strips of metals are bonded together, the two metals will expand or contract unequally, causing the bonded strip to bend. The bending of the strip can establish or disconnect a contact.

This contact could be an electric contact that operates a heating or refrigeration element, or, for example, a contact that opens or closes air dampers that control the intensity of a fire. An individual thermostat may differ from this description, but the underlying principle is the same. This chapter will briefly describe various systems that use a thermostat.

Perhaps the best known household example of a thermostatic system is the compressor refrigerator. The compressor reduces the temperature in the refrigerator to some pre-determined point. At that point, the contraction of the thermostat breaks the circuit and de-activates the compressor. The temperature increases; slowly if the door is closed, more rapidly if the door is open, until the expansion of the thermostat reconnects the circuit and activates the compressor.

The thermostat functions in a more sophisticated manner in most modern refrigerators. Not only does it control the refrigeration process, but it also controls the automatic defrost process. This is accomplished by different manners in different refrigerators. It reverses the compressor in some refrigerators, and activates a heating element in others. This function may be inversely related to the refrigeration function, whereby the activation of one, de-activates the other. It may also be time related, whereby activation is dependant upon time elapsed.

An ice maker works on a similar principle. The compressor freezes ice until the thermostat perceives the reduced temperature, indicating that the ice compartment is full. When ice is removed from the compartment, the temperature in the compartment increases. This increase is perceived by the thermostat which reactivates the compressor to freeze more ice.

A similar principle is used in a water cooler. New water replaces any cooled water drawn from the system. The new water raises the temperature of the water in the system. When the temperature rises to a given point, the thermostat activates the compressor to cool the water to a pre-determined temperature. A pressustat, which measures pressure the same way a thermostat measures temperture, can be added to this system to make soda water.

Water heating systems are the functional opposites of water cooling systems. There, too, new water replaces any water drawn from the system. This reduces the temperature of the water in the system. When the temperature falls below a given point, the thermostat activates a heater. This heater can be an electric heating element, or it may be fire that is controlled by air dampers that are opened or closed by the thermostat.

Similarly, whenever the temperature in an oven rises above a given point, the thermostat de-activates the heating element or closes the air dampers to the fire. Conversely, when the temperature falls to a predetermined level the thermostat reactivates the heating element or opens the air dampers.

In all the above systems, a variety of human actions causes activation and de-activation of the system. Consequently, it is necessary to determine which actions that affect the temperature are permitted on Shabbat and which are prohibited.

Chapter 2
Affecting the Thermostat and *Pesik Reisha*

Many actions can change the temperature perceived by the thermostat of a given system. If the change in temperature at a time when the system is inactive is sufficiently large, it can activate the system. The question is, to what extent is the person who changes the temperature responsible for the activation of the system.

This question is not affected by the amount of time that elapses between the action and the activation of the system. Thermostats generally respond slowly, and a relatively long period of time can pass between the initiation of a thermostatic reaction and its completion. An appropriate analogy for the action is shooting an arrow. Releasing a taut bow enables an arrow to travel through time and space and ultimately to damage property. Just as the releaser of the taut bow is responsible for the subsequent damage, regardless of the time elapsed,[1] so too the initiator of the thermostatic action should be responsible for the subsequent activation of the system, regardless of the time elapsed. Accordingly, any action that changes the perceived temperature sufficiently to activate the system, should be prohibited.

On the other hand, only those actions aimed at achieving the forbidden effect (*Melekhet machshevet*) are prohibited.[2] The actions that affect the perceived temperature are not aimed at activating the system (the forbidden effect), but rather, at adding or removing food (or water). As such they are *Melakha She'eino Mitkavein*, work not aimed at achieving a prohibited effect, which can be permitted on Shabbat.[3]

However, the performance of a *Melakha She'eino Mitkavein* that must inevitably cause a forbidden effect (*Pesik Reisha*) is nevertheless prohibited.[4] If the thermostat is close to the activation level, then any action that affects the temperature must inevitably directly activate the system. Accordingly, such action should be prohibited.

Yet, there is no way to determine in advance whether the thermostat is close to the activation level in which case activation is imminent. Each action, therefore, may or may not be the action that directly activates the system, and only the time of activation of the system demonstrates that the preceding action was the inevitable cause. This type of "inevitability," which can be determined only after the fact, is called a *Safek Pesik Reisha Le'She'avar*. The ruling for a *Safek Pesik Reisha Le'She'avar* is that if the result involves a Torah prohibition, the original action is prohibited; whereas if the result involves a Rabbinic prohibition, the original action is permitted.[5] Accordingly, affecting the temperature perceived by the thermostat should be permitted only when the resultant activation of the system involves Rabbinic prohibitions. (Examples of when Torah prohibitions are involved and when Rabbinic prohibitions are involved are discussed in Chapter 4).

Some contemporary Halakhic authorities, however, permit affecting the temperature perceived by the thermostat even when the resultant activation of the system involves Torah prohibitions. In their view, the *Pesik Reisha* activating the system is undesired, due to the financial and ecological wish to conserve energy.[6] An undesired *Pesik Reisha (Pesik Reisha De'Lo Nicha Lei)* is not prohibited if other lenient factors are involved.[7] In this case, the lenient factor of *Safek Pesik Reisha Le'She'avar* should combine with the *Pesik Reisha De'Lo Nicha Lei* to permit affecting the temperature even when Torah prohibitions are involved.[8]

Their premise, that activating the system is undesired, is questionable. Despite the fact that people do not wish to waste energy, they do use the various systems that refrigerate or heat. When the temperature change counters the function of the system, they do desire the activation of the system. The alternative, a cold heating system or a warm refrigeration system is certainly not desired, even if extra energy must be expended. Accordingly, the *Pesik Reisha* of activating the system seems to be a desired *Pesik Reisha (Pesik Reisha De'Nicha Lei)*.

In summation: affecting the temperature perceived by the thermostat is not intended to activate the system. Nevertheless, since affecting the temperature when the thermostat is not close to activation inevitably activates the system, it is forbidden when Torah prohibitions are involved, yet permitted when Rabbinic prohibitions are involved. This principle will be applied to specific actions in specific systems in chapter four.

Chapter 3
Actions that Lengthen an Existing Status

An underlying assumption of the preceding chapter is that the system involved is inactive at the time that the temperature is affected. Only then is it appropriate to discuss the "inevitability" of subsequent activation. Of course, if the action de-activates an active system the ruling is the same. But what if the system is active (or inactive) at the time that the temperature is affected, and the temperature change merely causes it to remain active (or inactive) longer? Does that permit affecting the temperature? If it does, then what if there is no way to determine whether or not the system is active? Is affecting the temperature under those circumstances also permitted?

Raising the temperature of an active cooling system (or lowering the temperature of an active heating system) does not change the status of the system. Had the temperature not been affected, the continued operation of the system would itself affect the temperature and de-activate the system. This de-activation is merely prevented by affecting the temperature in the opposite direction, which prevents the thermostatic circuit from opening. The closed thermostatic circuit can be viewed as a barrier to de-activation of the system. Accordingly, preventing the thermostatic circuit from opening prevents removal of the barrier to de-activation of the system. Preventing the removal of a barrier *(Meniat Ha'Meniah)* is a distant *Gerama* (See Section IV, chapter 6) that is permitted on Shabbat. Accordingly, since the activation of the system did not result from human action, and since the continued operation of the system results from *Meniat Ha'Meniah*, and no new action results, it is permitted to affect the temperature of the active system in this manner.

The situation is more complex when it is not known whether the system is active when affecting the temperature since that could activate an inactive system. Of course, if Rabbinic prohibitions are involved, affecting the temperature should be permitted, just as it is permitted to cause activation by affecting the temperature even when the system is inactive. If Torah prohibitions are involved, however, the possibility of transgressing a Torah prohibition should prohibit affecting the temperature when it is unknown whether the system is active or inactive. (Examples of when Torah prohibitions are involved and when Rabbinic prohibitions are involved are discussed in Chapter 4).

Nevertheless, another factor could permit affecting the temperature when it is unknown whether or not the system is active, in extenuating circumstances (such as having to remove food for a meal on a one time basis). This factor is another derivative of *Melekhet machshevet* (see chapter 2), that requires work to be done in its standard manner. Doing work in a non-standard manner (*Kil'achar Yad*) removes the Torah prohibition, although it is Rabbinically prohibited.[9] Accordingly, affecting the temperature in a non-standard manner never involves Torah prohibitions, and can consequently be permitted (at least on a one time basis) as discussed in chapter two.

Another powerful lenient factor combines with the above when the action affecting the temperature is opening the door to remove the food in the system, even when it is known that the system is inactive. In that case, unlike the case discussed at the end of chapter two, the subsequent activation of the system serves no purpose and is undesired. Consequently, when the system is inactive, and certainly when it is not known whether or not the system is active, affecting the temperature to remove all the food should be permitted.

In summation; affecting the temperature of an active system so that the system remains active longer, is permitted because it merely prevents the removal of the barrier to de-activation. It is not permitted to affect the temperature when it is not known whether or not the system is active (for a Torah prohibition). Nevertheless, under extenuating circumstances, it could be permitted to affect the temperature in a non-standard manner. However, the temperature may be affected even when the circumstances are not extenuating through an action that removes all remaining food.

Chapter 4
Conclusion

This chapter will apply the conclusions of chapters two and three to the systems described in chapter one, and will describe alternatives to the thermostat.

I. Refrigeration Systems

Two basic actions affect the temperature of the thermostat in a standard refrigerator: opening the door and placing warm food inside. The former action draws in the warmer outside air, and the latter action brings heat into the refrigerator. Either action can be done when the compressor is active since no Shabbat action is caused. The fact that the compressor is de-activated at a later stage is not considered a Shabbat action, as indicated in the previous chapter.

When the compressor is not active (activity of the compressor can be determined by its noise) the situation is more complex. Chapter two indicated that affecting the temperature under that condition is permitted only when the result involves Rabbinic prohibitions. In this case, the result (activating the compressor) is generally considered a Rabbinic prohibition,[10] although it is considered by some a Torah prohibition.[11] Accordingly, when the compressor is inactive many people only open the door of a refrigerator in a *Kil'achar Yad* manner, thereby avoiding the possibility of a Torah prohibition. *Kil'achar Yad* does not apply to placing warm food into a refrigerator, however, since food is normally placed in many different manners and since it involves a more direct action. Accordingly, placing warm food should be prohibited whenever the compressor is inactive.

The problem is reversed for automatic defrost refrigerators that work inversely to the compressor. *Closing* the door of the refrigerator when the compressor is *active* lowers the temperature which activates the defrost mechanism. Unlike the standard refrigerator, where opening the door directly increases the temperature, however, closing the door indirectly decreases the temperature by preventing the escape of the cold air. Nevertheless, when the prohibition involved is unquestionably a Torah prohibition, as, for example, when the defroster is a heating element that glows red, (See section IV) the door should only be closed in a *Kil'achar Yad* manner unless the compressor is inactive. Alternately, the solutions subsequently discussed for ovens may be adapted. (See III of this chapter).

Automatic defrost systems that are controlled by timers are less problematic. If the only relevant factor is time elapsed, then no action affects the defrost cycle, and only the regular refrigerator problems remain. On the other hand, if the timer measures the number of hours that the compressor is active, then each time the refrigerator is opened (which causes the compressor to be active longer) the time of activation for the defrost system is brought closer. Consequently, it would be preferable to always open the refrigerator in a *Kil'achar Yad* manner, specifically if the heating element glows red. Nevertheless, since the affect of the action is indirect, this system is Halakhically preferable to the above discussed defrost system inversely related to the cooling system.

A further complicating factor is present in "no-frost" systems. In these systems, a ventilator that generally either operates together with the compressor, or operates at all times, prevents frost buildup. To prevent warm air from being drawn in by the ventilator, it is de-activated when the door is opened. Since opening the door at that time directly de-activates the ventilator, it is prohibited on Shabbat. The only solution that permits opening the door when the compressor is active, for the type in which the ventilator operates together with the compressor, or to open at all for the other type, is to cover the switch that activates the ventilator with tape before Shabbat. The switch, normally released whenever the door is opened, is held back by the covering, and does not activate the fan. In all other respects, the no-frost refrigerator functions as does the automatic defrost refrigerator, and the conclusions of that discussion apply as well.

The problem of the ventilator, unique to the no-frost refrigerator, is similar to a problem shared by all refrigerators: The light. Opening the door releases a switch that opens a light, thereby transgressing a Torah prohibition. The solution discussed above, covering the switch with tape, solves this problem as well. Alternately, the bulb may be removed before Shabbat.[12]

The other systems based upon refrigeration, such as the water cooler, seltzer faucet, and ice maker, function in a manner similar to the standard refrigerator. Removing water or seltzer brings in warmer replacement water which is equivalent to placing warmer food into the refrigerator. Conversely, removing an ice cube is equivalent to opening the door of a refrigerator. The conclusions previously reached apply to these units as well.

II Heating Systems

The basic Halakhic difference between a heating system and a refrigeration system is that affecting a heating system generally involves the Torah prohibition of *Havarah*. As such, the *Safek Pesik Reisha Le'She'Avar* (see Chapter two) when the element is inactive involves a Torah prohibition, and the action of opening the oven door is prohibited. Ideally, therefore, food should be removed when the heating element is active. Food could, nevertheless, be removed from an oven whose heating element is inactive when all the food in the oven is removed, as discussed in chapter three. Otherwise, opening the door of an oven whose heating element is inactive can cause *Havarah* and should be prohibited except under extenuating circumstances in which the door could be opened *Kil'achar Yad*. Placing fully cooked food that is colder than the oven, inside the oven, however, could only be permitted when the heating element is active (See section I where it is demonstrated that this is usually prohibited because of the prohibition of *chazarah*).

Many thermostatically controlled gas ovens function in a manner that raises an additional problem. Opening this type of oven causes the fire to flare up. Since causing a fire to flare up transgresses the Torah prohibition of *Havarah*, such ovens may not be opened on Shabbat.

III Alternatives to the Thermostat

To avoid the problems discussed in this chapter, a simmerstat may be used in place of a thermostat. A simmerstat activates and de-activates a heating element at given times independent of the temperature in the unit. Accordingly, opening and closing the oven door has no effect on the unit and is permitted.

The temperature changes in a unit controlled by a simmerstat can be as high as 20^0C. These changes are usually not critical for an oven, but can spoil food in a refrigerator when the temperature is too high or when it freezes food that should not be frozen. Accordingly, the Institute devised a thermostat based upon the *Gerama* circuit described in Section IV.

Underlying this system is a capacitor designed to activate a system when fully charged. A second capacitor is designed to discharge the first capacitor by means of periodic pulses, before it fully charges.

As discussed in Section IV, the system can never be activated under those circumstances, since the activating capacitor is always discharged before it can activate the system. Instead of preventing the second capacitor from discharging the first by means of an extra prong, as was the case described in Section IV, the thermostat itself is designed to serve as the barrier. This thermostat should be in the closed position when there is sufficient heat (or cold) and should be designed to open when additional heat (or cold) is desired. In its closed position (i.e. when there is sufficient heat or cold) the activating capacitor is prevented from activating the system by the second capacitor. In its open position, however, the open thermostat acts as a barrier to the pulses of the second capacitor. Accordingly the first capacitor is not discharged and it can activate the heating (or cooling) system. Schematically it appears as follows in figure 5.1.

Affecting the temperature of the thermostat only opens the circuit of the thermostat.[13] This then acts as a barrier to the pulses that prevent the activating capacitor from activating the system. Section IV showed that erecting such a barrier is considered *Meniat HaMeniah* which is permitted for a Rabbinic prohibition. However, the Torah prohibition of *Havarah* is involved when using the thermostat for a heating element (whereas according to the *Chazon Ish* the Torah prohibition of *Boneh* is

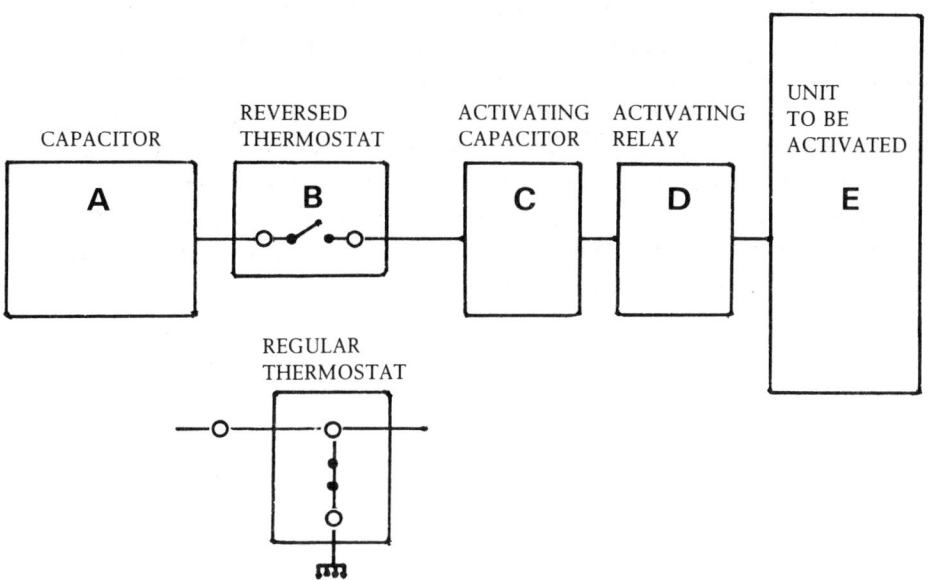

Fig. 5.1

When there is sufficient heat (or cold) thermostat (B) remains closed and allows pulses from capacitor (A) to discharge activating capacitor (C), thereby keeping the unit inactive. When there is insufficient heat (or cold) the thermostat (B) opens thereby preventing the pulses from capacitor (A) to reach the activating capacitor (C). As a result it can charge and activate the relay (D) which activates the system (E).

involved in any electrical circuit). Nevertheless, the factor of *Safek Pesik Reisha Le'She'Avar* mitigates the prohibition, thereby permitting an action that is *Meniat Hameniah*.

In summation: This chapter applied the conclusions of chapters two and three to the systems described in chapter 1. It was indicated that affecting the temperature in any system, but certainly in a heating system, is problematic when the system is inactive. The simmerstat, which is independent of any external temperature changes, was described as an alternative to the thermostat. Where the simmerstat is inapplicable, a thermostat in a *Gerama* circuit was described to reduce the direct effect of temperature changes on the system. One system not discussed was the water heating system. Due to the complexity added by the prohibition of *Bishul* that can be transgressed when heating the cold water, it is discussed in a separate section.

Section V

1. See for example *Nemukei Yosef*, Bava Kama 10A in the pages of the *RIF*, s.v. *Eisho*
2. TB Beizah 13b; *Rambam* Shabbat Laws 1:9
3. TB Beizah 23b; *Rambam* Shabbat Laws 1:5
4. TB Shabbat 75a; *Rambam* Shabbat Laws 1:6
5. The *Biur Halakha*, Orach Chaim 316:3 s.v. *Ve'Lakhen* says that according to the *Ramban, Ran* and Me'iri it is permitted even for a Torah prohibition. The *Taz* 316:3 & 4 seems to permit it as well. The *Shulchan Arukh HaRav*, Orach Chaim 257 Kuntres Aharon cites the views of *Rashi* and *Rambam* that a *Safek Pesik Reisha* is prohibited, and concludes that this view should be followed for a Torah prohibition
6. Rabbi S.Z. Auerbach in *Mazkeret*, 5732 P.74 and *Talpiot* VII 1 & 2; Rabbi S. Zelig in *HaPardes* 5694 VIII 3:14; *Ziz Eliezer* 8:12; etc.
7. *Mishnah B'rurah*, Orach Chaim 321:57
8. Especially since there are views that permit each individually
9. TB Shabbat 92a
10. As in note 55 of Section IV
11. As in note 56 of Section IV
12. Although both solutions are acceptable, the former is preferred because there is not even electric potential in the circuit
13. The result of opening a thermostat, which directly closes no electric circuits, is preferrable to the result of closing a thermostat which could be a problem according to the view of the *Chazon Ish*

SECTION VI

Hot Water Systems

Introduction		169
Chapter 1	General Hot Water Systems	171
Chapter 2	Hot Drinking Water	177
Chapter 3	Coffee and Tea Machines	189
	Yerushalyim, Nisan 5745	
	Yerushalyim, Tishre 5746	

Introduction

The widespread use of hot water for a multitude of purposes has become an integral feature of modern life. Various devices, ranging from gas and oil boiler systems to electric percolators, supply this hot water. Many serious Halakhic problems arise when using these systems on Shabbat.

Among these problems is maintaining large quantities of hot water, which can transgress the prohibitions of *Shehiyah* and *chazarah*, as discussed in section one. Another problem, thermostatic control, was discussed in the previous section. Perhaps the most serious problem, however, is that of *Bishul*, which can be involved whenever water is heated on Shabbat.

The Institute for Science and Halakhah developed various systems to solve these problems. Chapter one indicates the problems associated with hot water systems for general use, and explains the Halakhic basis for two alternate systems developed by the Institute. Chapter two discusses the two relatively inexpensive systems that supply large quantities of Halakhically acceptable hot drinking water on Shabbat. Chapter three explains the additional problems involved in brewing fresh coffee and tea on Shabbat, and describes three systems developed by the Institute to solve those problems.

Chapter 1
General Hot Water Systems

Various types of hot water systems are used to produce hot water for general use. At the heart of these systems is a tank into which cold water enters to be heated, and from which hot water is drawn. To maintain constant water pressure, any hot water removed from the system is generally replaced simultaneously with cold water. This water is generally heated to a predetermined level by means of a thermostat.

Two problems result from using such systems on Shabbat. The first problem is that heating cold water on Shabbat transgresses the Torah prohibition of *Bishul*. This problem is not solved by heating the water before Shabbat, since each use of hot water on Shabbat draws cold water in its wake to replace it. This cold water is heated by the hot water in the tank, if not by the heat source that heats the water in the tank. In either case *Bishul* occurs, since the hot water, itself heated by fire or its Halakhic equivalent, is a *Toldot Ha'Ur* (a subcategory of fire) which transgresses *Bishul* just as the heat source does (See section IV). Since the cold water is drawn into the system as a direct result of using hot water, the user of hot water is directly responsible for the *Bishul* of that water.

The second problem is that of thermostatic control, discussed in the previous section. As indicated there, each use of hot water is a *Safek Pesik Reisha Le'She'Avar* which is prohibited for Torah prohibitions. In this case, the operation of the heating element (or increase of fire) involves the Torah prohibition of *Havarah*. Consequently, the use of hot water is prohibited in these circumstances.

The solution to these problems lies in arranging circumstances so that neither the Torah prohibition of *Havarah* is involved nor the

Torah prohibition of *Bishul*. The first problem, removing the Torah prohibition of *Havarah*, was solved in Section IV by using a heating element that does not glow red. Accordingly, the *Safek Pesik Reisha Le'She'Avar* involves a Rabbinic prohibition, which, as indicated in the previous section, is permitted. On the other hand, the problem of *Bishul* remains, since even if *Bishul* by a heating element that does not glow red is Rabbinic, it is prohibited and no *Safek Pesik Reisha Le'She'Avar* is involved. Conseqently, the use of a hot water system heated by a heating element that does not glow red is also prohibited.

The problem of *Bishul* may be avoided by not heating the water to the temperature that constitutes *Bishul*. The temperature that constitutes *Bishul* for a liquid is the temperature that causes the human hand to recoil (*Yad Soledet Bo*).[1] It is difficult to determine the precise temperature in which that occurs, but it can safely be said that a human hand will not recoil from temperatures below 45^0C.[2] If a 3^0 margin of safety is added as protection against technical problems such as voltage and gas flow changes then the thermostat may be set at 42^0C. Heating water to 42^0C by means of a heating element that does not glow red transgresses no prohibitions, yet, the water is warm enough for most household uses.

If the problem of *Bishul* is solved by heating the water to 42^0C, however, then a heating element that does not glow red is unnecessary, provided that the thermostat is modified to solve the problem of *Havarah*. The previous section demonstrated that a thermostat could be modified so that its effects are independent of human action, and that it could consequently be used on Shabbat. If the thermostat described there closes the circuit at temperatures *above* 42^0C, and opens the circuit at temperatures *below* 42^0C then hot water from such a system could be used on Shabbat even if heated by a standard heating element. The reasons for this permission are discussed in the previous section.

This system is unnaceptable for circumstances in which there is a genuine need for very hot water. A possible solution for such circumstances is to divide the functions of hot water storage and hot water production, and to make the two functions independent of each other. This can be accomplished by dividing the boiler into two vats, one for boiling the cold water and one for storing the hot water. The boiling of the water and its transfer to the storage vat are controlled by a pre-set automatic time clock. The storage vat can be designed that the pressure is maintained through air pressure so that using hot water does not cause the entry, and subsequent heating of cold water.

A further problem remains, however. Varying amounts of cold water are generally mixed with the hot water to achieve the desired temperature when using the hot water. This mixing, however, can transgress the prohibition of *Bishul*. To solve this problem, the tube connecting the two vats can be constructed from heat resistant polyprophylene. Since that absorbs no heat from the hot water flowing through it, it functions as a divider between the two vats. Accordingly, the storage vat can be considered a *Kli Sheni* whose water may be mixed with cold water to cool the hot water (See section III).

This system automatically heats cold water at given intervals and transfers it to the storage vat automatically. Whenever hot water is transferred to the storage vat, cold water is drawn into the heating vat. Nevertheless, the entry of this cold water and its subsequent heating is relatively indpendent of the use of hot water.

On the other hand, this independence is itself problematic from a practical view point. Large quantities of hot water could overflow during lower than normal demand periods. Similarly, during greater than normal demand periods there could be insufficient hot water.

This problem can be solved by combining two previously discussed principles. The first principle, *Meniat Ha'Meniah* (See section IV) allows transfer of hot water, when needed, in a manner not Halakhically attributable to the user of the hot water. This can be accomplished by adding both an electric float valve between the two vats and an electric timer to delay the opening of the valve. If after any delay cycle the float falls to a preset point, indicating insufficient hot water, the float valve circuit opens. This open circuit prevents the timer from delaying the opening of the valve. On the other hand, as long as the float is above the pre-set point, the timer will continue to delay the opening of the valve. Consequently, whereas hot water enters the storage vat (drawing in cold water to be heated in the heating vat) when needed, the use of the hot water does not directly cause cold water to be heated. It only lowers the float which causes the circuit to be open. This

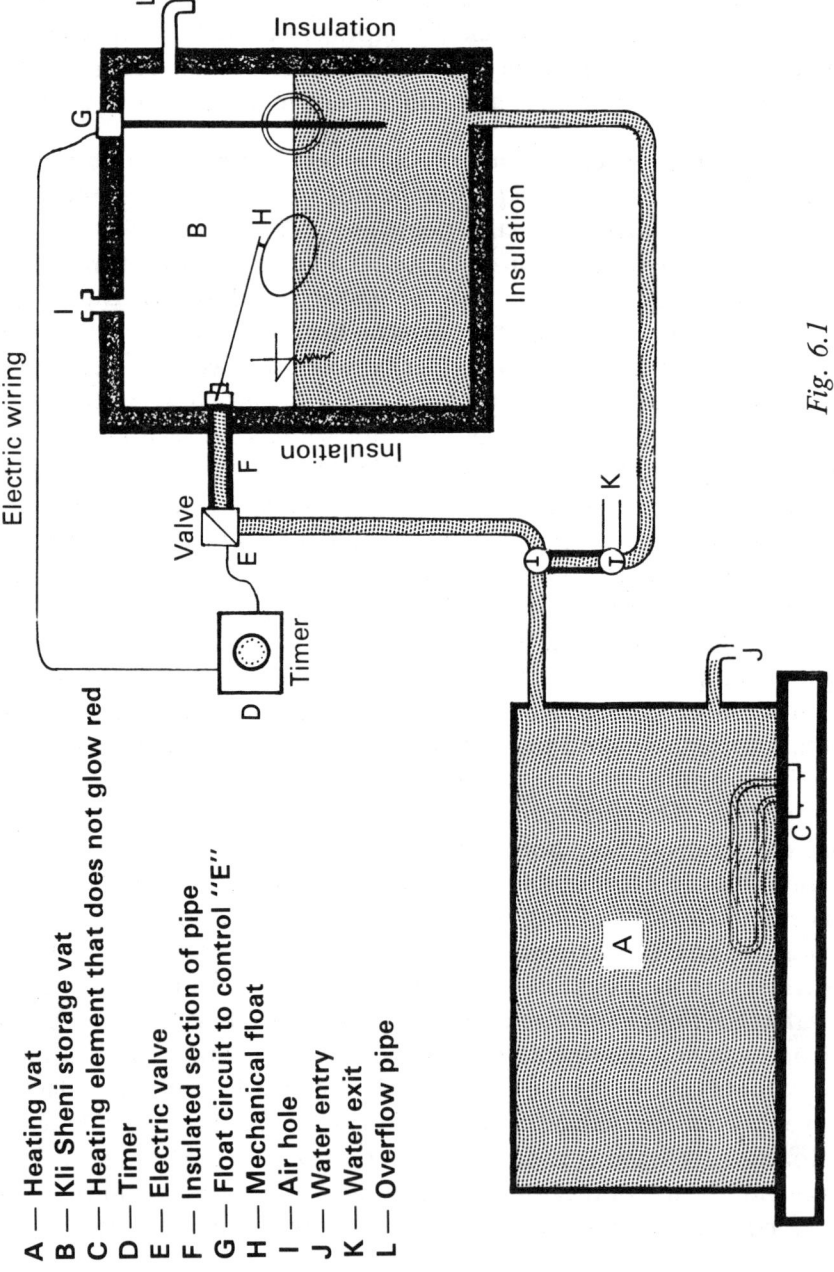

A — Heating vat
B — Kli Sheni storage vat
C — Heating element that does not glow red
D — Timer
E — Electric valve
F — Insulated section of pipe
G — Float circuit to control "E"
H — Mechanical float
I — Air hole
J — Water entry
K — Water exit
L — Overflow pipe

Fig. 6.1

merely prevents the timer from delaying the opening of the valve. Accordingly, this system should be permitted, based upon the previously discussed permission for *Meniat Ha'Meniah*, since ach use of water involves a *Safek Pesik Reisha Le'She'avar*. See section V chapter 4.3.

The second principle, a heating element that does not glow red, strengthens this permission. Since, as indicated in Section IV, heating water with a heating element that does not glow red is a Rabbinic prohibition, the cold water drawn into the heating vat by *Meniat Ha'Meniah* involves *Meniat Ha'Meniah* for a Rabbinic prohibition which should certainly be permitted.[3] See figure 6.1.

As discussed previously, the connection between the two vats should be constructed from polyprophylene so that the storage vat could be considered a *Kli Sheni*. Another helpful modification is to add a mechanical float valve to the electric valve to prevent a malfunctioning valve from opening when there is sufficient hot water. It is also advisable to provide for overflow storage in case this too fails.

Additional technical and Halakhic material on these systems may be found in *Chimum Mayim BeShabbat* published by the Institute for Science and Halakhah.

Chapter 2
Hot Drinking Water

The systems described in the previous chapter are unacceptable for the production of hot drinking water for Shabbat both for a technical and a Halakhic reason. The technical reason is that the hot water pipes of the above system as well as general systems are not suited for drinking water. The Halakhic reason is that it is prohibited to use water from a drinking water system if use will trigger any valve that causes water to be heated, as is the case in the previous system. This differentiation is based upon the relative sizes of the two systems. Whereas the size of the previous system is generally large enough to mitigate the interest in additional quantities of hot water, the size of hot drinking water systems is small enough to desire the heating of additional water.[4] In addition, there is no need to design the system as a *Kli Sheni*, since any addition of cold water for drinking takes place in a cup, itself a *Kli Sheni* (as opposed to mixing hot and cold water directly from the tap).

As in the previous system, one chamber in this system thermostatically heats cold water which is then transferred to a second chamber for storage and use. However, the use of hot water may not cause the heating of new cold water in this system. On the other hand, to avoid having too much or too little hot water at a given time, constantly varying quantities of cold water must be heated.

These apparently conflicting goals may be achieved by using a system based upon the law of connecting vessels (with modifications that will be subsequently described). According to that law, the level of a liquid in two connecting vessels will tend to equalize. Accordingly, if the heating chamber and storage chamber are connected, the levels of the two chambers will equalize after each use of hot water. At that

Fig. 6.2

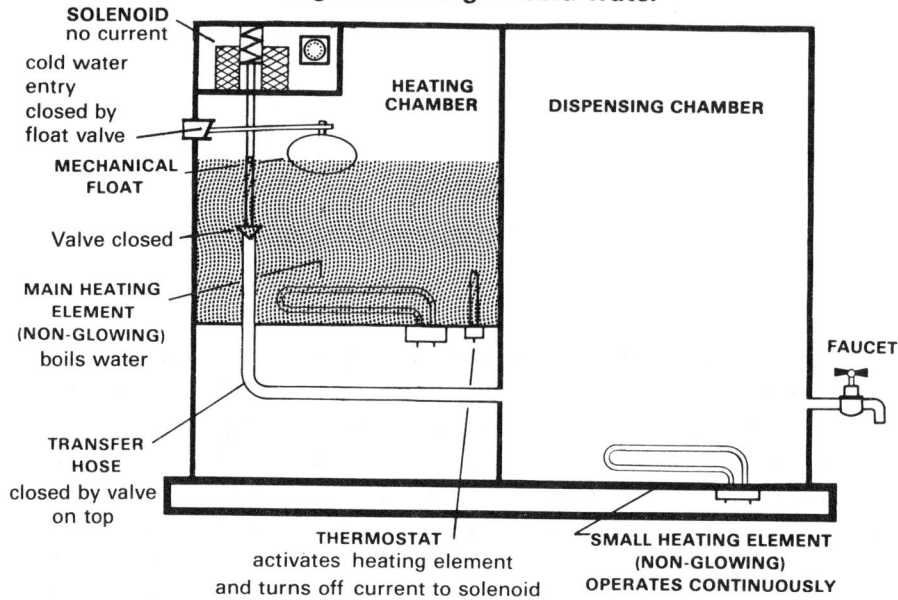

Proceed to Stage II or Stage IV

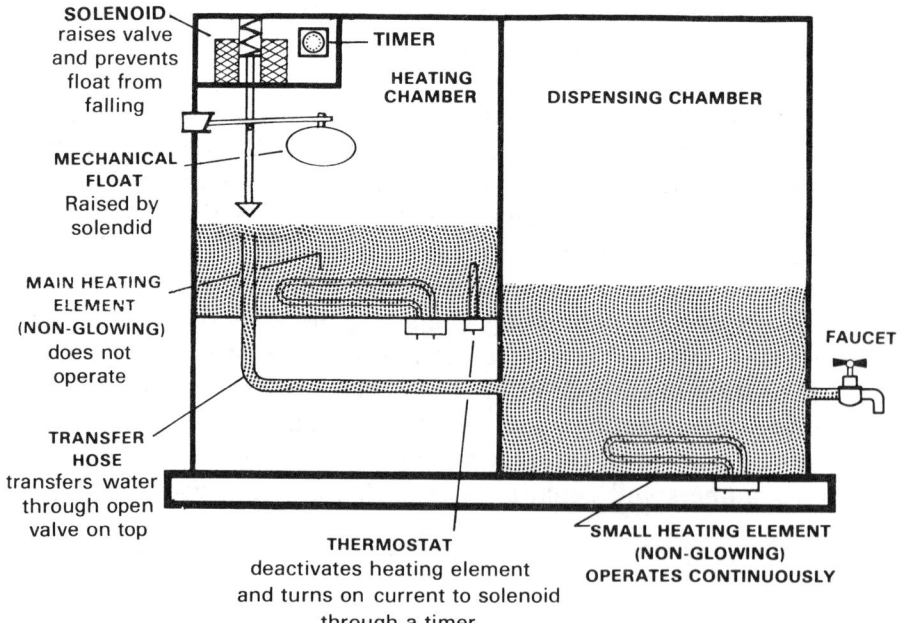

Proceed to Stage III

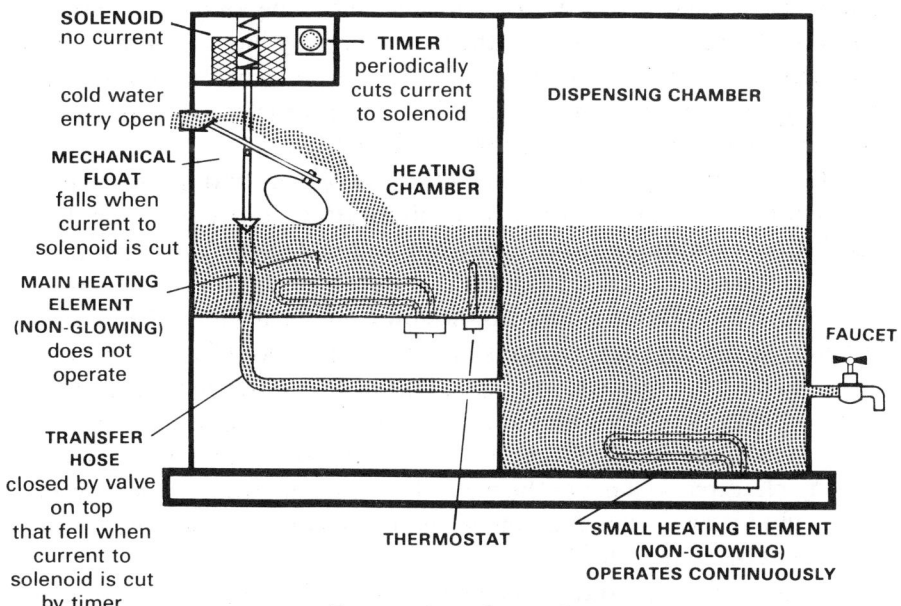

Proceed to Stage I

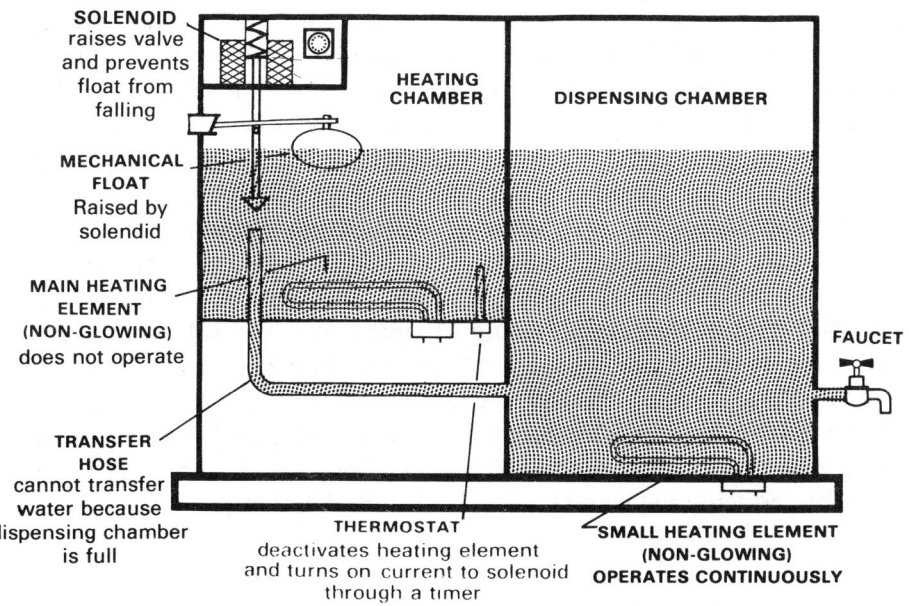

When water is drawn from dispensing chamber proceed to Stage II

point there seems to be two alternatives. The first alternative is continued use of hot water, thereby lowering both levels without replacing the depleted water, until there is no more hot water. The second alternative is to replace any hot water transferred to the storage chamber with cold water that will be heated.

Both alternatives are unsatisfactory, however, and do not achieve the conflicting goals. The first alternative, especially for large institutions, results in insufficient hot water. On the other hand, the second alternative can transgress the Torah prohibition of *Bishul*.

A third alternative similar to the solution discussed in the previous chapter, is to arrange circumstances so that cold water enter the heating chamber relatively independent of hot water use. A relatively constant supply of hot water can nevertheless be produced by using (as a first step) a mechanical float bar valve that allows cold water into the heating chamber whenever the water level falls below a predetermined point. However, in this manner, using hot water can once again cause the *Bishul* of cold water.[5]

To prevent this, and nevertheless maintain a relatively constant supply, the following may be done: (See figure 6.2) A thermostat in the heating chamber should control both a heating element in the heating chamber and a solenoid for the storage chamber. Whenever the heater operates, the solenoid should not, and vice versa. The solenoid should have two functions. The first is to magnetically raise the valve that closes the connection between the two chambers, and the second is to prevent the float bar in the heating chamber from falling along with the water level as the heated water transfers to the other chamber.

These modifications have the following effect: When cold water enters the heating chamber the reduced temperature perceived by the thermostat causes the operation of the heating element. When the temperature of the water reaches the desired level, the thermostat opens the heater circuit, thereby stopping its operation, and closes the solenoid circuit, thereby initiating its operation. The solenoid opens the valve between the two chambers, allowing the water levels to equalize, and simultaneously prevents the float bar in the heating chamber from falling. This second function is necessary to insure that using hot water while the valve between the two chambers is open (thereby reducing the water level in both chambers) does not cause new cold water to enter the system. However, if no new cold water enters the system, the supply of hot water could be finished before the temperature of the heating chamber falls sufficiently for the thermostat to stop the operation of the solenoid.

To prevent this, a timer attached to the solenoid circuit, periodically cuts the current, thereby closing the valve between the two chambers, and allowing the float bar in the heating chamber to fall. If at that time the water level in the heating chamber is low, the external valve allows cold water to enter. This cold water lowers the temperature in the heating chamber causing the thermostat to close the heating circuit and to open the solenoid circuit. Conversely, if when the timer allows the float bar to fall the water level is too high for the external valve to open, no cold water enters, the thermostat does not operate the heater, and the timer can restore the current to the solenoid. Continued use of hot water lowers the hot water level in the two chambers. Consequently, each time the timer cuts the current, the float bar falls lower than the previous time until the external valve opens and cold water enters the system to repeat the process.

Each use of hot water in this system is several steps removed from heating cold water. The first step is lowering the water level, without which no new water can enter. As long as the heater operates, however, the water level in the heating chamber remains constant. After the operation of the heater, the solenoid prevents cold water from entering the system. Only after the timer cuts the current to the solenoid can the float bar fall and open the cold water valve. Then, however, the valve between the two chambers is closed and using hot water does not cause cold water to be drawn in. Thus, using hot water never directly causes cold water to be heated.

Nevertheless, the inevitable result of using hot water in a system this size is the entry and *Bishul* of cold water. Since an inevitable result, *Pesik Reisha* (See Section V), is prohibited, this system should be prohibited. Yet, a *Pesik Reisha* is only prohibited when the actions leading to the inevitable result are themselves prohibitable. In this case the "actions" are the removal of the "barrier" of water, the "barrier" of the valve between the two chambers, and the "barrier" of the cold water valve. Each of these "barriers" is removed by means of a *Gerama* (See figure 6.3). Consequently, the permissibility of this system is

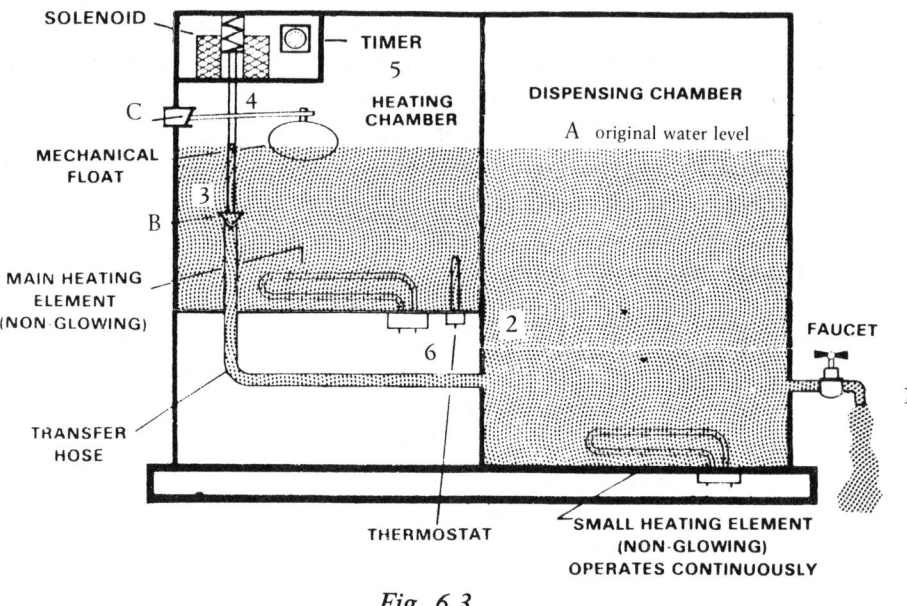

Fig. 6.3

1. Hot water is drawn from storage chamber.
2. This allows water from the heating chamber to enter the storage chamber but...
3. Water could only enter B when valve is raised by solenoid.
4. When the solenoid raises the valve it also raises the float bar which prevents cold water from entering.
5. When the timer cuts the current the solenoid allows the float bar to fall to the water level thereby opening the cold water valve. Only then can water enter.
6. To be thermostatically heated.

A, B, and C represent barriers that must be removed before cold water can enter to be heated.

dependent upon the permissibility of a *Pesik Reisha* resulting from these interacting *Gerama*s.

As discussed in Section II, it is Rabbinically prohibited to do a *Gerama* of a Torah prohibition on Shabbat. Accordingly, the permissibility of a *Pesik Reisha* resulting from three interacting *Gerama*s can be derived from the permissibility of a *Pesik Reisha* resulting from three interacting Rabbinic prohibitions.

One such example is removing on Shabbat a knife stuck into a barrel before Shabbat. The *Shulchan Arukh* permits this despite the fact that removing the knife inevitably broadens the hole which can transgress the Torah prohibition of *Boneh*[6] (Building — the broadened hole facilitates storage in the barrel). The *Magen Avraham* bases this permission on the interaction of three mitigating factors, each of which would be Rabbinically prohibited alone. The three factors are: The action is done to remove the knife and not for the sake of making a hole (*Eino Tzarikh Le'Gufo*); broadening the hole in this case is destructive (*Mekalkel*); and the hole is not made in the standard manner (*Kil'achar Yad*).[7]

There are other examples, however, that are prohibited despite the presence of the same three factors. One such example is dragging heavy furniture along unpaved ground. The inevitable result, a furrow, can also transgress a Torah prohibition. Nevertheless, despite the facts that the furniture is not dragged for the sake of the furrow, that making the furrow is destructive, and that the furrow is not made in the standard manner, the *Magen Avraham* himself prohibits the dragging.[8]

The *Tehillah Le'David* attempts to reconcile this apparent discrepancy based on the rulings of the *Tosfot Shabbat*[9] and the *Shulchan Arukh HaRav*.[10] They permit broadening an existing hole but prohibit opening a new hole. Accordingly, removing the knife, which merely broadens an existing hole can be permitted, whereas dragging heavy furniture, which opens a new furrow, is prohibited.

But why is broadening a hole under these circumstances less severe than opening a new hole under the same circumstances? Both directly broadening a hole and directly opening a new hole can transgress a Torah prohibition. If so, then why is there a differentiation with respect to the Rabbinic prohibition of the latter?

A possible answer, says the *Tehilah Le'David*, is that even when three mitigating factors combine, an action can be prohibited if the results of the action are manifest. In other words, dragging a heavy piece of furniture can be prohibited due to the resultant new furrows which makes it *appear as if* a prohibited action occurred. On the other hand, removing the knife from the barrel causes no apparent change. Consequently, the three mitigating factors can permit the removal.[11]

If this logic is accepted, then using the water heating device described above is analagous to removing the knife from a barrel. Using hot water has no apparent connection with the subsequent *Bishul* of cold water. Certainly, the three *Gerama*s separating the use of hot water from the *Bishul* of cold water should be at least as permissible as three mitigating factors that are Rabbinic prohibitions. Whereas *Gerama* is permitted to prevent loss,[12] a Rabbinic prohibition is not. Thus, if three mitigating factors that are Rabbinic prohibitions permit an action whose results are not apparent, then using the above described water heater should certainly be permitted.

Even if this logic is not accepted, one further modification in the system can make the heater fully permitted. If the heating element does not glow red, then, as discussed in Section IV, the resultant *Bishul* involves a Rabbinic, rather than Torah, prohibition. *Gerama* of a Rabbinic prohibition was also shown to be permitted by most authorities. Certainly, three combined *Gerama*s of a Rabbinic prohibition should be permitted.

An alternate system, based upon similar Halakhic principles and using a heating element that does not glow red, can be designed around a standard electric percolator. A standard percolator has an internal and an external water chamber. Cold water enters into the external chambers and is heated to approximately 80^0C. At that point the water passes into a special tube that contains powerful heating elements that boil the water. The pressure resulting from boiling the water forces the water into an internal chamber. At that point, additional cold water is drawn in to continue the process until a given water level is reached.

To adapt this system to Shabbat use, the following adaptations must be made, for reasons that will subsequently be explained. Firstly, the heating elements should not glow red, as mentioned above. Secondly, two electrodes, one at the maximum water level and one at the minimum water level, should be designed into the external chamber. Thirdly, there should be holes between the two chambers just above the level of the uppermost electrode for overflow (See figure 6.4).

As in the previously described system, no water can enter during the operation of the heating element. Since water is transferred by means of the heating element, the transfer does not directly bring cold water in its wake. Similarly, the use of hot water, which allows hot water to be transferred into the internal chamber, does not directly bring cold water into the system.

The system works as follows: Cold water enters the external chamber through an electric valve controlled by the electrodes. When the water level reaches the top electrode it opens the valve circuit (closing the valve) and closes the heating circuit (activating the heating element). The pressure of the boiling water in the small area of the tube forces hot water into the internal chamber. As more water is forced into the internal chamber the water level of the external chamber falls. The level continues to fall until the level of the bottom electrode is reached. At that point, the bottom electrode opens the heating circuit (de-activating the heating element) and closes the valve circuit (opening the valve and drawing in cold water). The process is then repeated.

This process continues to repeat whether or not hot water is drawn from the internal chamber. If no hot water is drawn, then when the level in the internal chamber reaches the level of the holes between the two chambers, the hot water overflows back into the external chamber and no new cold water enters (See figure 6.4). Thus, using hot water does not directly cause cold water to enter and be heated but merely prevents the water in the internal chamber from overflowing back into the external chamber. Had this not been prevented it would in turn have prevented the falling of the water level. Had the level not fallen to the level of the bottom electrode, it would have prevented cold water from entering. In other words, using hot water does not allow it to prevent the water from overflowing, which does not allow the water to prevent the level from falling, which does not allow the water to prevent the entrance of cold water.

This is called *Meniat Hameniah* (see Section IV) which was shown to be permitted on Shabbat, with respect to a heating element that does not glow red.

Fig. 6.4

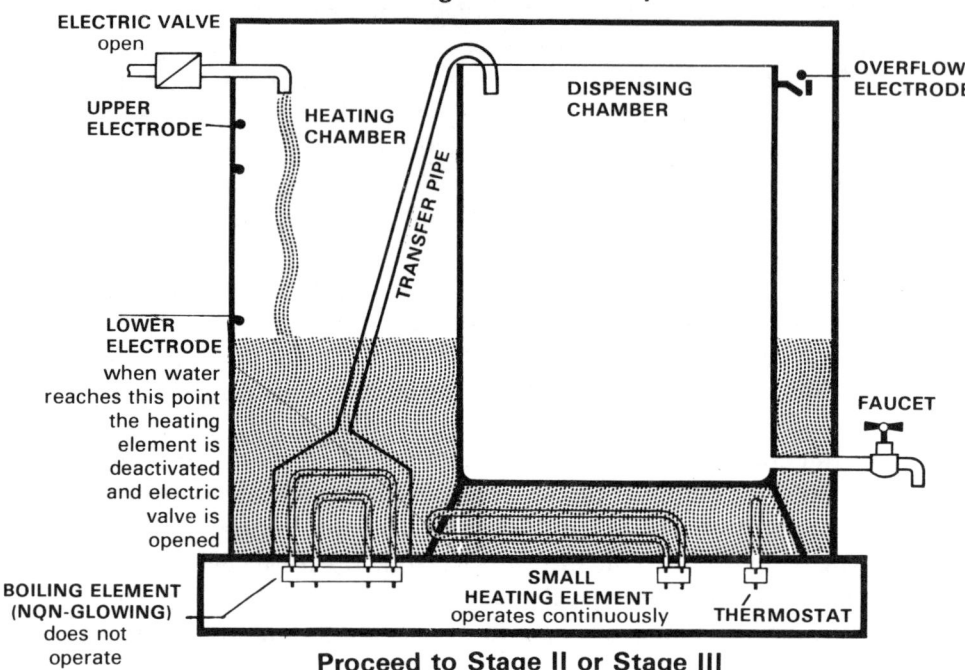

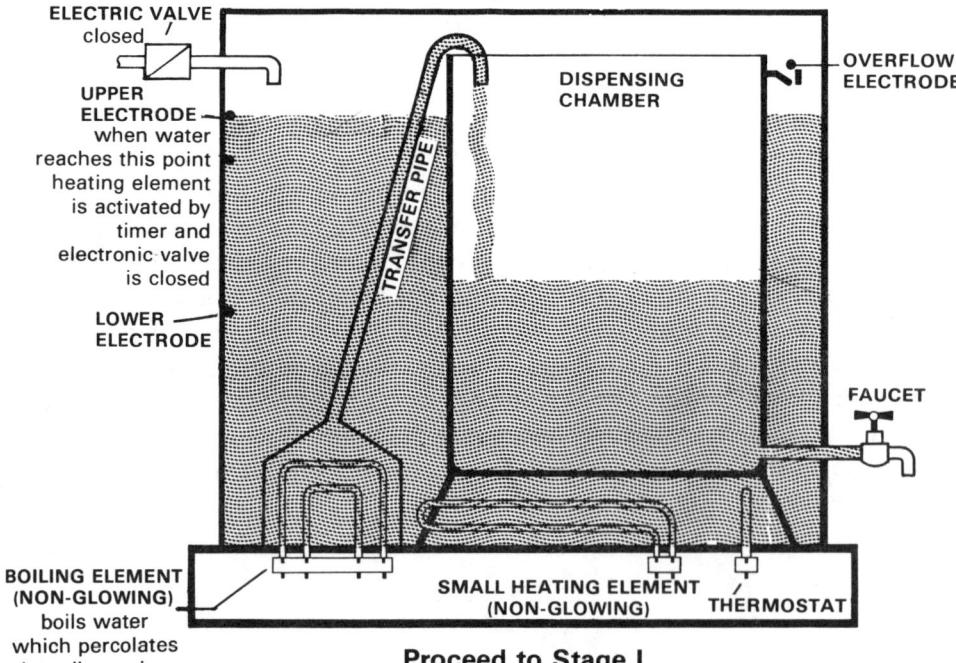

Stage III: Overflow

Repeats until water is drawn from dispensing chamber (Stage IV)

Stage IV: Use of water

Proceed to Stage II

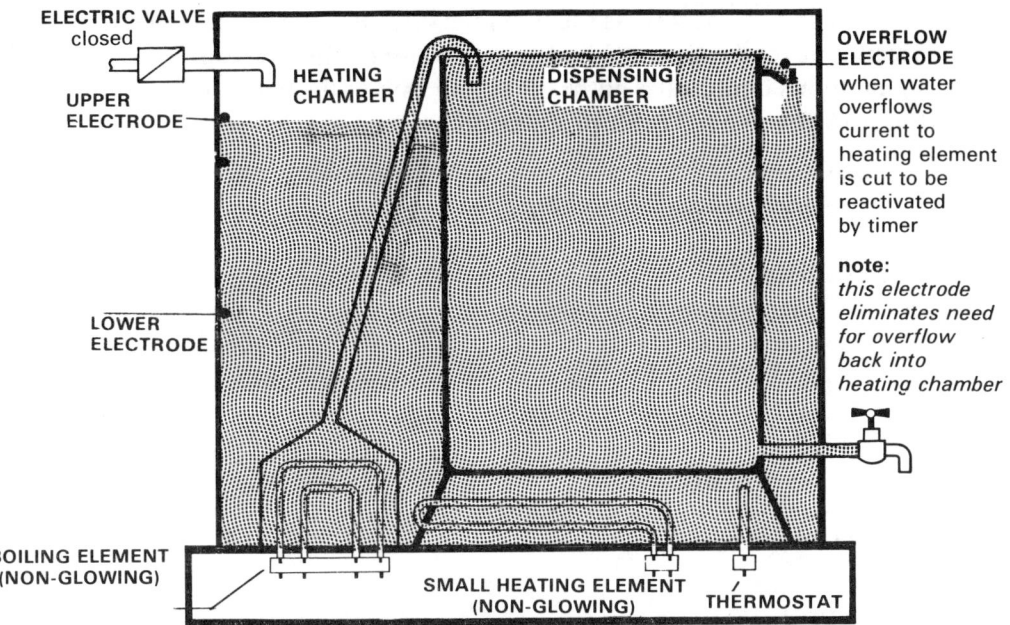

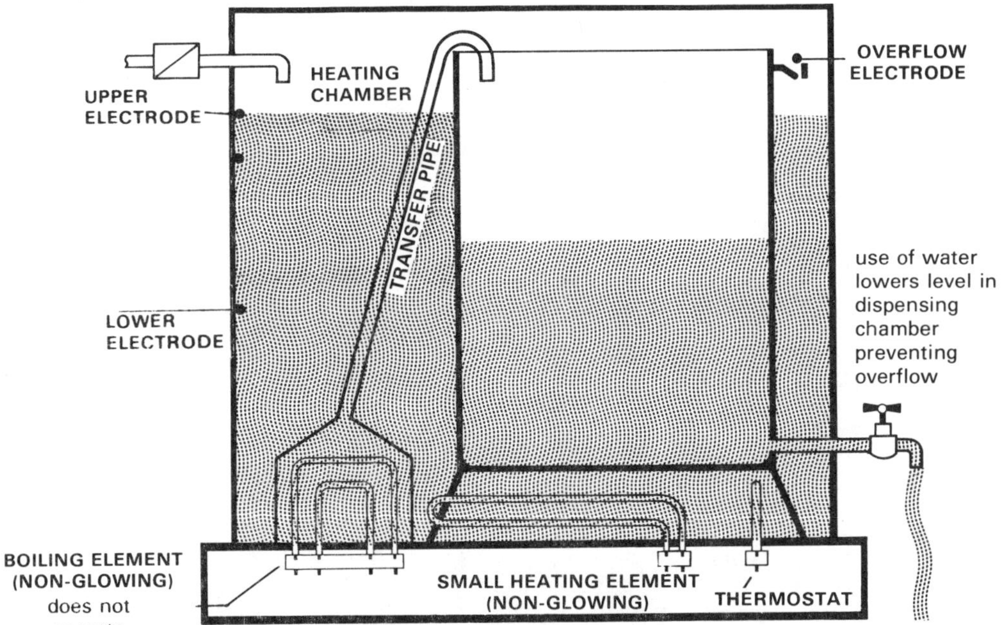

This system, as well as the previous system, have been shown to be acceptable for producing hot drinking water on Shabbat. Of course, no signal lights could turn on or off at any part of the process, since that, too, can involve a Torah prohibition.

Chapter 3
Coffee and Tea Machines

Producing Halakhically acceptable hot drinking water on Shabbat, in the manners described in chapter two, does not solve the problem of producing hot coffee or tea on Shabbat. Both hot coffee and hot tea are generally made by brewing the coffee grind or the tea leaves in hot water. Although the production of that water is permitted in the manner described above, the brewing process, as will become apparent, could involve prohibitions relating to *Bishul*.

Strictly speaking, the brewing process cooks — *Bishul* — the leaves or the grind, thereby imparting their flavor to the hot water. Although it is permitted to re-cook previously cooked dry food (See Section I for Rabbinic prohibitions that may be involved), coffee grind and tea leaves are dry foods that were roasted. Does the permission for re-cooking a cooked dry food apply to roasted dry food as well?

The *Shulchan Arukh* cites two views on this point:
"Some say that a baked or roasted food that is subsequently boiled in liquid involves *Bishul*, and [thus] it is prohibited to place bread even into a boiling *Kli Sheni*. Others permit."[13]

The *RaMA*, in his glosses on the *Shulchan Arukh* explains what the *Shulchan Arukh* means by "others permit":
"[Others permit placing bread] into a *Kli Sheni*. Others, [adds the *RaMA*] permit this even into a *Kli Rishon*. And it is customary to take precautions to avoid placing bread into even a *Kli Sheni* whose temperature is *Yad Soledet Bo*."[14] (See chapter 1)

The phrase "customary to take precautions to avoid" (*Nohagim Le'hizaher Le'khat'chilah*) implies that it is permitted by the letter of the law, but customarily avoided. If so, then placing roasted food into a *Kli Shlishi*, which, as discussed in Section III, is considered by most authorities more lenient than a *Kli Sheni*, should certainly be permitted. Indeed, this conclusion is supported by the rulings of the *Pri Megadim*[15] *Shulchan Arukh HaRav*,[16] *Mishnah B'rurah*,[17] and *Ketzot Ha'Shulchan*.[18]

Even the *Chazon Ish*, who does not differentiate between a *Kli Sheni* and a *Kli Shelishi* of equivalent temperatures could permit placing roasted food into a hot *Kli Shelishi*. The determinant factor for prohibitions, in his view, is the temperature of the water. However, although he rules that anything considered *Bishul* in a *Kli Sheni* is considered *Bishul* in a *Kli Shelishi* as well, roasted food is not considered *Bishul* even in a *Kli Sheni*. Rather says the *Chazon Ish*, it is "only a restriction accepted by custom which applies only to that which custom restricts."[19] By implication, since custom does not restrict roasted foods in a *Kli Shelishi*, he permits placing roasted food (such as coffee) into a *Kli Shelishi*.

Accordingly, the hot water for a coffee (or tea) brewing system that may be used on Shabbat should have the status of hot water from a *Kli Shelishi*. If a standard coffee urn is connected by means of prophylene tubing to the hot water system described in chapter one of this section, then the water in the urn can be considered *Kli Shelishi* water. The external cold water that winds through the coiled tube to the coffee grind (as is the case in a standard coffee urn) is heated by a *Kli Shelishi*. That water may then filter through the coffee grind to produce fresh coffee that may be used on Shabbat.

The system described above is relatively speaking quite primitive. The water from the *Kli Sheni* system enters through a manual valve, rather than an electric valve, since electric circuits can close as a direct result of using coffee in a system containing electric valves. In addition, the urn can have no active heating elements, since that transforms the urn into a *Kli Rishon* (See section III). This raises the problem of heat maintenance; the longer the brewed coffee remains in the urn, the colder it becomes.

Both these problems can be solved through the methods described in chapter one. A thermostat, electric valves and a timer delay circuit can be added to this system. The thermostat should control the timer delay circuit which is connected to the electric valves. As long as the thermostat keeps the circuit closed the timer will periodically delay the opening of the valves so that they remain closed. When the temperature falls below a preset limit the delay circuit is opened and the valves are no longer prevented from opening. Hot water from the *Kli Sheni* boiler can then enter the external chamber of the coffee machine and the colder water can drain through another valve. When the temperature rises sufficiently the thermostat recloses the circuit and the valve is again cyclically prevented from transferring water. Similar methods may be used to maintain constant quantity. (The Halakhic rationale for these methods are discussed in chapters 1 and 2).

This system combines principles of *Kli Sheni* with principles of *Gerama*. An alternate system is based upon principles of *Gerama* only. In such a system, the external chamber can have a heating element that does not glow red and its use, as will become apparent, can be permitted.

A heating element, as mentioned above, generally makes the urn a *Kli Rishon*. However, a *Kli Rishon* which can cook and transgress the prohibition of *Bishul*, can only refer to a vessel cooked by fire or its derivatives. Since Section IV showed that a heating element that does not glow red is neither fire nor its derivative, it cannot make the urn into a *Kli Rishon*. Furthermore, the two views in the *RaMA* concerning the permissibility of placing roasted food into a *Kli Rishon* discussed above, apply only to direct placement. Since even the stringent view considers direct placement a Rabbinic prohibition, *Gerama* of that placement should be permitted by the many authorities who permit *Gerama* of a Rabbinic prohibition (See Section II). If it is *Gerama* of placement into a vessel heated by an element that does not glow red (which is thus not a true *Kli Rishon* and in which, presumably, direct placement is less stringent) it should certainly be permitted.

This permission applies to brewing the coffee through *Gerama*. Cold water (as opposed to the roasted coffee or tea) heated in this manner involves *Gerama* of the Torah prohibition of *Bishul* and should be prohibitied. On the other hand, as indicated in Section II, reheating water that is still hot is permitted. In accordance with these principles a standard coffee urn may be adapted in the following manner:
The external chamber should have a thermostatically controlled heating element that does not glow red. It should be filled and heated

before Shabbat, and the thermostat, modified by a timer delay system as described in the previous chapters, will maintain the proper temperature on Shabbat. The *Kli Sheni* boiler described in chapter one is attached by means of polyprophylene tubing to the coiled tube that leads to the coffee grind.[20] The water can be of lower temperature than the water in the external chamber, and it will be heated by passing through the coils. The water should enter by means of a timer delay system, as described in the previous chapters, that closes the circuit when the brewed coffee falls below a certain level, and opens it above a higher level. There should be at least a two liter differential between the two levels, so that each use of coffee does not directly cause entry of new water. In addition, the coffee grind should be placed into the system at a time when there is no water passsing through. Thus, when water subsequently passes through the grind, it is not a direct result of the previous action.

Actually, if *Gerama* is the basis for the permission, then a third simpler system is possible. Either of the drinking water systems described in chapter two may be attached to the internal tube of a coffee urn. The water entry, temperature maintenance and coffee grind placement is as described for the second system of this chapter.

The second system is preferable to the third system because the hot water of the second system might still be considered *Kli Shelishi*. The *Magen Avraham* writes that when water in a *Kli Sheni* is transferred back to the original *Kli Rishon* it is still considerd a *Kli Sheni*.[21] In this case, then , the water entering the urn should still be considered a *Kli Shelishi* since it enters the urn from a *Kli Shelishi*. The fact that the urn has a heating element that does not glow red need not make the urn a *Kli Rishon*, as indicated above. On the other hand, the water in the third system cannot be considered a *Kli Shelishi*, and the entire basis for permission is *Gerama*.

In summation: Coffee (or tea) can be freshly brewed automatically on Shabbat with three systems. The first and preferred system uses *Kli Shelishi* water for brewing and *Gerama* principles for other problems. The second system brews through *Gerama* as well, with water that is presumably considered *Kli Shelishi*. The third, least preferred system is based fully on *Gerama*.

Section VI

1. TB Shabbat 40b
2. Rabbi S.Z. Auerbach in *Noam,* Vol. VI; the temperature given in *Igrot Mosheh,* Orach Chaim Volume 4:74 is 110°F which falls within the margin of safety discussed here
3. This is better than a Gerama of a Rabbinic prohibition discussed in Section II
4. Thus a *Pesik Reisha De'Nicha Lei* could be involved
5. Since drawing hot water below that point directly pulls in cold water to be heated
6. *Shulchan Arukh* Orach Chaim 314:1
7. *Magen Avraham* Orach Chaim 314:5
8. *Magen Avraham* Orach Chaim 337:1
9. *Tosfot Shabbat,* Orach Chaim 314
10. *Shulchan Arukh HaRav,* Orach Chaim 314:3
11. *Tehila Le'David* Orach Chaim 314:3
12. See Section II
13. *Shulchan Arukh* Orach Chaim 318:5
14. *Rama,* Orach Chaim 318:5
15. *Pri Megadim,* Eshel Avraham 318:35
16. *Shulchan Arukh HaRav* Orach Chaim 318:11
17. *Mishnah B'rurah* 318:47
18. *Kezot HaShulchan* 124
19. *Chazon Ish,* Orach Chaim 58:9; also see 52:19
20. To make the coiled tube a *Kli Shlishi*
21. *Magen Avraham,* 257:14

SUMMARY

BRIDGING THE GAPS AND REINFORCING THE WALL

by Chaim Friedberg

The Approach

Modern technology affords us a variety of improved devices and facilities, many of which, however, present operational problems in connection with Shabbath, kashruth, medicine and other commandments of the Torah. Undertaking the challenge of providing solutions to such problems — and, thereby, facilitating and enhancing observance of Torah and mitzvoth — the Institute for Science and Halacha has achieved considerable success. The subject of this volume is but one of the various areas demonstrating these achievements.

Devices have been developed, aimed at eliminating the influence of the individual on actions which are forbidden on Shabbath. In some cases, this is done by replacing a human activation with an automatic one. In others, a melachah (work which is forbidden on Shabbath) is accomplished in a manner which isolates the individual involved from the results of his action, to the extent that the action is not attributed to him at all.

Doubts

This approach may arouse some questions:

- Doesn't this approach circumvent Torah observance and create a breach in the fortress of religious law?
- Didn't our sages forbid circumvention of Torah law in several places in the Talmud and adopt preventive measures against its use?

A primary objective of the Institute is to facilitate the planning and maintenance of urgent and essential activities such as medical and security services on Shabbath, by various technological means. This is intended to minimize the need to resort to special exemptions (heterim) provided, regarding Torah prohibitions, in cases where danger of life (pikuaḥ nefesh) is involved, and, regarding rabbinic decrees, where there may be considerable financial loss (hefsed merubeh) or pressing circumstances (she'at hadeḥak).

But, one may ask, what justification is there to seek other methods and avoid utilitizing the heter of pikuaḥ nefesh? After all, whatever one does on Shabbath is not only permited, it is obligatory! And, we must set aside Shabbath laws in such circumstances.[1]

It is correct, of course, that saving a life supersedes all Shabbath prohibitions, and that, furthermore, it is then a mitzvah to perform all otherwise prohibited acts.[2]

Halachic Obligation To Plan Ahead

It should be kept in mind, however, that this law applies only at the time of the incident, when life is already in danger. But, when we know of the situation sufficiently in advance, there is a clear obligation to plan ahead so as to avoid having recourse to the heter of pikuaḥ nefesh. Commenting on the obligation of an adult Jew — in particular — to violate Shabbath for a critically ill person, the Rama, for example, quotes the opinion that, if it is possible to act without delay, it is preferable to do so by means of a shinui or by having a gentile perform the melachah.[3]

Regarding a person who undertakes a caravan journey through the desert, where it is common knowledge that he will be forced to desecrate Shabbath in order not to be left behind alone in the desert on Shabbath, the Shulḥan Aruch states that it is forbidden to start out within three days before Shabbath.[4]

The Mishnah Berurah quotes the opinion brought by Knesseth Hagedolah in the name of Ridbaz, that if he knows for sure that he will be forced to voilate Shabbath, he is forbidden to go altogether.[5]

Magen Avraham quotes the opinion of Sefer Ḥasidim that a woman in her ninth month of pregnancy must prepare everything before Shabbath, so that she will not have to violate Shabbath in case the birth occurs on Shabbath.[6]

Although the Shulḥan Aruch makes it clear that a critically ill person can be fed forbidden food on Yom Kippur, if no permissible food is available, he cautions that if there are two types of forbidden food there, the patient should be fed the less severely prohibited food first.[7]

The Ḥatam Sofer wrote that we are obligated to make all arrangements before Shabbath for a woman after childbirth, for an ill person or for circumcision, in order to avoid violating Shabbath; although, if preparations were not made in advance and the situation occurs on Shabbath, swift action, as required, is praiseworthy.[8]

These statements of leading halachic scholars elucidate our obligation — to the extent we find it possible — to make such advance preparations as are necessary, in order to prevent violation of Shabbath or avoidable utilization of the heter of pikuaḥ nefesh. Such advance planning may include:

- analysis and planning of activities so as to substitute permissible actions for forbidden ones;
- reverting from manual activation to various automatic activations;
- restricting violatory activities either quantitatively or qualitatively; for example, by reducing the severity of an activity from a Torah prohibition to a rabbinic prohibition.

Health Care

As reflected in statements brought from Shulḥan Aruch, Rama, Mishnah Berurah, Knesset Hagedolah, Ridbaz, Magen Avraham, Sefer Ḥasidim and Ḥatam Sofer, the obligation to plan ahead, in order not to resort to the heter of pikuaḥ nefesh, applies to individual cases. How much more important is prior planning for Shabbath observance in public institutions, where there may be — or are often likely to be — multiple instances of pikuaḥ nefesh!

There are additional conclusive reasons why careful and thorough planning of Shabbath activities in health care and other insitutions is vital:

- The vast majority of activities — even in hospitals — are not matters of life or death.

- The scores of routine activities performed daily in all types of institutions include some which can be dispensed with on Shabbath. For others — though it is important they be done — performance by their routine procedure may involve unjustified violation of Shabbath.

- A Torah observant patient, not aware of the nature of his condition, may be terribly distraught at the knowledge of Shabbath desecration in his behalf, and his precarious condition is liable to worsen due to his pain and anguish over this.

- Providing means which are permissible for serving patient needs on Shabbath, under *all* circumstances, will assist in relieving unnecessary stress upon both patients and staff, without compromising whatsoever the quality of patient care.

If both critical and non-critical activities are performed on Shabbath in a permissible manner, then:

- Doctors, nurses and other paramedical or assisting personnel will be freed of the burden of repeated determinations as to whether they *must* or *may not* desecrate Shabbath.

- Patients will not be upset by learning, or assuming, that their condition is critical, when they observe that Shabbath is being desecrated in their behalf.

Bridging The Gap In Industry

Total interruption of operation of certain industrial plants, or, at least, operation of some of their continuous processes, would result in heavy financial loss or total shutdown. Shabbath desecration in such cases is unavoidable, to our great dismay, unless changes are developed and implemented.

Other technological innovations must be introduced so that continued standby operation is independent of manual activation and that no activation is attributable to individuals.

The concern for elimination of the obstacles of strict prohibitions, and guidance regarding halachically oriented procedures are among the most vital objectives being tackled by the Institute.

* * *

In a foreword to Maaseh Ḥoshev,[9] responsa on contemporary halachic problems, Rabbi Levi Yitzḥak Halperin analyzes differences between Torah and secular systems of law, as well as differences between those Torah laws addressed solely to the Jewish people as "am segulah' (Shabbath, for example) and those Torah laws which, in addition, advance the goal of perfecting the universe (tikkun ha'olam) and assuring the peace and welfare of mankind.

The conclusions of this study, derived from a broad spectrum of authoritative sources,[10] relate intimately to the issue at hand:

- The 613 commandments were given to the people of Israel in view of their special virtue as the chosen people of the Creator.

- The performance, or lack of performance of a commandment by a Jew, therefore, relates to the doer, rather than to its having been done.

- Furthermore, the expanded sanctity resulting from a Jew's performance of a commandment, or its reduction due to a transgression, emerge from the virtue of the doer and not from the result of the act.

- With respect to punishment for a crime such as murder, where the perfection of the world is at stake, Torah law requires that a murderer be punishable by death, even if he only caused death indirectly (grama). Although, in the case of grama, beth din was not given the power of sentencing a Jew to death, he is nevertheless considered guilty at the hands of Heaven.[11] [12]

- Regarding Shabbath, the Torah focuses its demands on the *action* of the Jew, since Shabbath laws are concerned solely with the virtue of the Jewish people, and not at all with the purpose of perfecting the world.

- Therefore, in Torah law, grama is permissible with respect to melachah on Shabbath, since, as stated in Gemara Shabbath[13] ... it is written, 'You shall not *do* any work';[14] it is *doing* that is forbidden, grama is permitted. But our sages forbade grama as well, lest one come to do work directly with his own hands, without grama.

- The prohibition is, then, against a Jew *doing* work on Shabbath; the intent of the Torah is not that work not be done on Shabbath.

- For, according to Torah law, it is permissible for a Jew to have a gentile do all types of work for him on Shabbath.

- Our sages forbade telling a gentile on Shabbath to do work or benefitting from work a gentile does on Shabbath.

- Where, however, no instruction to a gentile or benefit from his work is involved, it is permissible to place a pot of raw food on the stove before Shabbath or to set animal, bird or fish traps before Shabbath, even though the actual work — the cooking or the trapping — occurs on Shabbath.

- In summary, it evolves that the commandments are addressed mainly to the Jewish people because of their virtue and the Creator's love for them, in order that they elevate themselves by doing the positive commandments and not deteriorate by transgressing the negative commandments. The intent of the Torah is not to negate the execution itself.

An often repeated expression of this latter concept appears in the final passage of Mishnah Makkoth:[15] 'Rabbi Ḥananyah, the son of Akashya says, 'The Holy One, blessed be He, wanted to bestow favor on Israel, and therefore gave them an abundance of Torah and commandments, as it was said, 'The L-ord desires his (Israel's) righteousness in order that He magnify and glorify the Torah.'

* * *

It follows from these sources and many others, that in the appoach adopted by the Institute for Science and Halacha there is no exploitation of a breach or loophole in halachah. As faithful Jews, we firmly believe that the laws of the Torah are the laws of G-d, as Moshe Rabbenu said to Yithro, 'I make them know the statutes of G-d and His laws.'[16]

Just as He did not leave anything lacking in the universe which He created, so, He left nothing lacking in his Torah. And, where He left another way, this was done with a special intent. That our sages found it proper to forbid things that the Torah did not forbid, this was done with the sanction of the Giver of the Torah. That which the Torah itself did not forbid, but allowed the sages to forbid, is founded on the Torah's intent that this prohibition *not* be a Torah prohibition, but rather only a rabbinic prohibition — with the stringencies (ḥumroth) and leniencies (kuloth) denoted thereby.

However, where the Sages did not prohibit something, it is certainly permissible even initially (lechatḥila), and there is no justification to forbid it.

Deceit versus Inventiveness

We find various types of circumvention. Some of these were prohibited by our sages, but some are permissible. There are some cases of evasion which — since they are tantamount to deceit and lying — are forbidden. There are other types of evasion, however — characterized by cunning and inventiveness only — which circumvent a prohibition without coming into contact with it, and are permissible.

The Rambam,[17] Tosefoth Yom Tov[18] and Rabbi Ya'akov of Lisa[19] discuss the distinction between various types of evasion.

1. In the forbidden, deceitful type of evasion, Rabbi Yaakov writes, the deed is a forbidden act and the doer, intending to accomplish this act, does it while attempting to conceal that he is doing — or is interested in — the prohibited act. The Gemara Shabbath[20] offers four such examples:

- one who prepares new liquor on Ḥol Hamo'ed, on the pretense that he has no liquor, although some of his old stock still remains. Under these actual circumstances he would be prohibited from making new liquor on Ḥol Hamo'ed.

- one who hangs up a strainer on Yom Tov, purportedly to put pomegranates in it (which would be permissible), and then puts dregs in it to be drained (which is forbidden).

- one who plugs a piece of garlic into a hole in a barrel, purportedly to hide it (which would be permissible), but in reality seals a leak in the barrel (which is forbidden).

- one who, supposedly unwittingly, goes to sleep in a ferry boat docked on one side of a river, and, after the boat has been ferried to the other side of the river by a gentile on Shabbath, goes out and surveys the fruits of his vineyard there.

In each of these examples, the doer performs a forbidden action, without appearing to intend that it be done. Such evasion is defineable as deceit, which was not permitted by the Sages, except with respect to rabbinic prohibitions.

2. On the other hand, where the deed succeeds in avoiding completely a forbidden act, such evasion is not prohibited at all, but can be defined as inventiveness which is permitted by halachah. A well known example of this is the sale of ḥametz to a gentile. Regarding the prohibition to even *see* ḥametz on Pesaḥ, the Sages postulate that you may not see *your* ḥametz, but you may see that of a gentile. Therefore, of what concern is it whether one intends to purchase the ḥametz after Pesaḥ or not?

Where an evasive action is done in accordance with halachah, it is clearly not forbidden at all.

Returning, then, to the doubts expressed at the beginning of this discussion, there need be no concern of prohibition in the exploitation of technological inventions in keeping with halachah, since no deceitful evasion is involved. This approach utilizes technological innovations in an inventive way, in order to circumvent halachic prohibitions, by applying grama in a permissible manner.

Enhanced Observance Of Shabbath

It should be further emphasized that this approach is aimed at improving and enhancing Shabbath observance. Following the guidelines set by the Institute for its activity, devices are *not* developed for human comfort or pleasure, nor to allow the use of things we would otherwise refrain from using. Items developed by the Institute have been based on the primary objective of solving existing problems.

The proposed solutions *avoid* the need:
- to perform the relevant actions in a forbidden manner on Shabbath;
- to arrive at dangerous situations;
- to forego extremely essential needs on Shabbath.

Opinions Of Recent Gedolim

The revered Hazon Ish discusses in depth various applications of the Shabbath use of automated technological arrangements.

The activation of an electrical hotplate to heat Shabbath food by means of a timeclock preset before Shabbath, and milking cows by means of an automatic milking machine, concludes the Hazon Ish,[21] are permissible, provided attention is given to removal or avoidance of related problems, such as attribution of an act to an individual; electricity production without Shabbath violation; shehiyyah and hazarah prohibitions).

There is *no* expression of fear in the writings of the Hazon Ish, however, of thereby circumventing halachah, or a resultant breach in the wall of Shabbath observance. Rabbi Shlomo Frankfurter of Berlin[22] writes of the approval given by leading rabbinic authorities to the use of an electric hotplate on Shabbath, once the questions of bishul, shehiyyah, hazara, and the like are resolved. Among the authorities whose agreement he cites on this subject were leading rabbis in Poland and Hungary, including Rabbi M. Palatzki (author of Keli Hemda and Hemdat Yisrael) and the Grand Rabbi of Munkacz (author of Minhat Elazar.[22] These scholars, as well, were not deterred by a danger of evasion or breach in the wall of Shabbath.

Recognition Of Leading Torah Scholars Today

The efforts, activities and solutions developed by the Institute to strengthen and facilitate Shabbath observance have earned the recognition and esteem of the Torah world. Leading poskim have not only given approval of the Institute's activities, but also refer their questioners to the Institute in all halachic matters related to technology.

* * *

May it be His will that no mishap occur as a result of our work, that we not stumble in any matter of halacha, and that we be among those who bring benefit to the community by magnifying and glorifying Torah.

Notes

1. Beth Yosef, Oraḥ Ḥayyim 328, ד"ה והיה
2. Rambam, Hilchoth Shabbath 3:3
3. Oraḥ Ḥayyim 328:12
4. Oraḥ Ḥayyim 248:4
5. Oraḥ Ḥayyim 248:4, Mishnah Berurah 26
6. Oraḥ Ḥayyim 330, Magen Avraham 1
7. Oraḥ Ḥayyim 618:9
8. Responsa Ḥatam Sofer, Yoreh De'ah 338, ד"ה גם מ"ש
9. Maaseh Ḥoshev, responsa on contemporary halachic problems, by Rabbi Levi Yitzḥak Halperin, Institute for Science and Halacha, Jerusalem, 1985
10. a. Sanhedrin 59:1
    b. Sanhedrin 56
    c. Ramban, Vayyishlaḥ 34:13
    d. Rambam, Hilchot Melachim 9:14
    e. Responsa, Rama 10
    f. Mishnah Gittin 8:2
    g. Rambam, Hilchot Sanhedrin 20:7
    h. Sanhedrin 107:2
    i. Sanhedrin 66, 67
    j. Rambam, Hilchot Rotzeaḥ Ushemirath Nefesh, Chapter 3
    k. Rambam, Hilchot Melachim 9:4
    l. Ramban, Bereshit, Vayyeshev 37:26
    m. Rambam, Hilchot Melachim 10:2
    n. Rambam, Hilchot Yesodei Hattorah 5:1
11. Rambam, Hilchot Yesodie Hattorah 5:10
12. Vayyikra, Kedoshim 19:16.
13. Shabbath 120:2
14. Shemoth, Yithro 20:10
15. a. Mishnah Makkoth 3:16
    b. Rambam, Commentary on Mishna Makkoth 3:16
    c. Yesha'yah 42:21

    d. Malbim, Shemoth, Yithro 19:5
    e. Devarim, 'Ekev 7:6, Reeh 14:2
16 Shemoth, Yithro 18:16
17 Rambam, Commentary on Mishnah Temurah 5:1
18 Tosefoth Yom Tov, Mishnah Temurah 5:1
19 Mekor Ḥayyim, Hilchot Pesaḥ 448:11
20 Shabbath 138:2
21 Ḥazon Ish, 38, Oraḥ Ḥayyim
22 Otzar Ḥayyim, Part 5, Page 89.